Introduction to
and Ear Training

Introduction to Sightsinging and Ear Training

Second Edition

Bruce Benward
University of Wisconsin, Madison

Maureen A. Carr
The Pennsylvania State University

J. Timothy Kolosick
University of Arizona

 Brown &
Benchmark

Book Team

Developmental Editor *Deborah Daniel Reinbold*
Production Coordinator *Kay Driscoll*
Permissions Editor *Gail Wheatley*

WCB Brown & Benchmark

A Division of Wm. C. Brown Communications, Inc.

Vice President and General Manager *Thomas E. Doran*
Executive Managing Editor *Ed Bartell*
Executive Editor *Edgar J. Laube*
Director of Marketing *Kathy Law Laube*
National Sales Manager *Eric Ziegler*
Marketing Manager *Kathleen Nietzke*
Advertising Manager *Jodi Rymer*
Managing Editor, Production *Colleen A. Yonda*
Manager of Visuals and Design *Faye M. Schilling*

Production Editorial Manager *Vickie Putman Caughron*
Publishing Services Manager *Karen J. Slaght*
Permissions/Records Manager *Connie Allendorf*

Wm. C. Brown Communications, Inc.

Chairman Emeritus *Wm. C. Brown*
Chairman and Chief Executive Officer *Mark C. Falb*
President and Chief Operating Officer *G. Franklin Lewis*
Corporate Vice President, Operations *Beverly Kolz*
Corporate Vice President, President of WCB Manufacturing *Roger Meyer*

Copyeditor *Siobhan Drummond*

Consulting Editor Frederick W. Westphal, California State University, Sacramento

Library of Congress Catalog Card Number: 91–73082

ISBN 0–697–10642–X

Printed in the United States of America by Wm. C. Brown Communications, Inc., 2460 Kerper Boulevard, Dubuque, IA 52001

10 9 8 7 6 5 4 3 2 1

Contents

Unit 4

Unit 5

Preface to the Student

The Goal of Sightsinging and Ear Training

While being able to sing unfamiliar melodies at sight or write them down from dictation is certainly an important goal, it is, surprisingly enough, only a means to an end. The more important goal is to look at a score of music (any music) and be able to hear it in your mind without having to sing or play it out loud. That accomplishment is put to practice as a daily routine by members of a professional symphony orchestra who must look over their parts only minutes before a crucial rehearsal—no time for long practice sessions. The conductor of the orchestra must be prepared to spot pitch and rhythmic errors instantly (ear training). This phenomenon is known by some as a "hearing eye" or "seeing ear" and by others as "aural imagery." By whatever name it is known, it is the supreme goal of this text.

Sightsinging and ear training are so closely related to aural imagery that the two are nearly inseparable, and indeed, this combination is one of the few known ways to develop aural imagery. In addition, singing out loud or writing dictation is essential because it is the only process by which you can communicate your progress to your instructor.

The Need for a Strategy

Singing melodies or writing dictation from this text without any thought whatsoever might prove successful if you select melodies from the first few chapters. But initial success will soon turn sour when you tackle ensuing units, and the errors made the first week will still be there in the sixth week and the twelfth week. In order to make improvement, a strategy (a way to improve) is an absolute necessity. Guessing may suffice for amateurs but not for professionals.

Helpful Strategies for Sightsinging and Ear Training

1. Syllables or Numbers. Learn thoroughly whatever syllable or numbering system your instructor recommends. To take the guesswork out of sightsinging and ear training it is imperative that you "know" the scale degree of all melody notes and communicate that information to your instructor, as well as to yourself.

2. Intervals. Knowing what E sounds like when you are presently singing C is something to get accustomed to. At first it may be difficult, but when you learn that from C to E is the same distance as from F to A or G to B your problem is diminished considerably. Learning to sing and identify intervals (distance between pitches) is an absolute must.

3. Familiarity with the Scale. Figure out the key and identify the scale before trying to sing or take a melody from dictation.

4. Reference Tones. Isolate the 1st, 3rd, and 5th scale degrees of the key and sing them until memorized. Then, for a while at least, circle all 1st, 3rd, and 5th scale degrees in the melody. These are called reference tones, and you can easily relate all other scale degrees to 1, 3, or 5.

5. Tonic Pitch. You should be able to pause anywhere in a melody and sing the tonic (1st scale degree) pitch immediately. Try it a few times just to make sure you can do it. This skill applies to both sightsinging and ear training.

6. Mind Singing. Practice scanning melodies by thinking rather than singing what each pitch sounds like. In ear training try to visualize sounds: Place each pitch on an imaginary staff. The sooner you can do this, the closer you are to the real goal of sightsinging—aural imagery.

7. Steady Tempo. Avoid starts and stops in sightsinging. Doing so means that the tempo you selected may be too fast—your voice gets ahead of your mind.

8. Rhythm. In sightsinging, trying to figure out the next pitch and rhythm at the same time may be overwhelming at first. Before singing, tap out the rhythm of the entire melody. In ear training, some students find it easier to get the pitches down on paper first, then concentrate on the rhythm as a separate operation. This divide and conquer technique will help considerably, and you will soon be able to coordinate both. Remember that much can be learned from mistakes in the early stages of ear training and sight-singing skills. Carefully analyze the problem, alter your strategy, and try again! Persistence and effort bring success.

Acknowledgments

Thanks go to the following people who reviewed this manuscript in various stages of development: Mary A. Burroughs, East Carolina University; Gary Karpinski, University of Oregon; Sandra Matthes, Liberty University; Tressa Reisetter, No school affiliation; Rodney Rogers, Arizona State University; Robert A. Stephenson, Northern Michigan University; Nancy E. Whitman, Kearney State College; Stephen Yarbrough, University of South Dakota; Janis Watkins, Southwestern Baptist Theological Seminary.

. . . . . . **1** . . . . . .

A. SS Rhythm: One-, Two-, and Three-Beat Values

I

Consider each number (ending with a double bar) as a module to be sung separately or as part of a series.

1. Clap or say (on a neutral syllable like "ta") each bar, repeating it several times until you can achieve at least a moderate tempo.
2. If your instructor recommends, conduct yourself using the hand movements shown on page 2.
3. When each measure is well within your grasp, try an entire line, performing all modules one after the other.
4. Accuracy is the prime goal—speed (fast tempo) is desirable, but not absolutely essential at the moment.

Beat of 2   Beat of 3   Beat of 4

II

Sing the following exercises on a neutral pitch, observing the rhythm only:

1. Clap the meter.
   Sing the rhythm (using numbers).
2. Say the meter (using numbers).
   Clap the rhythm.
3. Tap the meter with one hand and the rhythm with the other.
4. Half the class taps the meter while the other half claps the rhythm.

B. ET Rhythmic Dictation: Full-Beat and Half-Beat Values

Each exercise consists of a two-measure melody. Complete the rhythm (only) of each exercise on the lines provided below.

1. As you hear the preparatory measure(s), count the meter. If the meter is 4/4, count 1–2–3–4.
2. After the first hearing: Say or clap the rhythm immediately.
3. After the second hearing: Say meter beats and clap rhythm immediately. If you are sure of the rhythm by now, write it on the appropriate line.
4. If a third hearing is needed: Use it to verify rhythms you have written down or to clear up any misconceptions.

Listen to the rhythm as many times as needed to get the right answer! Do it in three hearings if you can, but accuracy is the most important item for the moment.

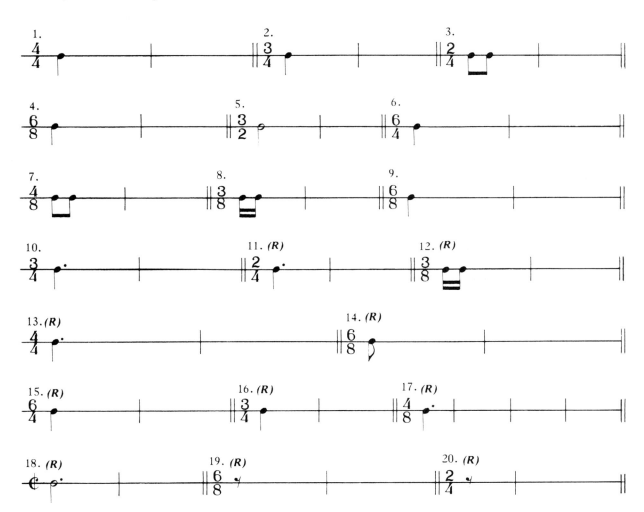

C. SS Diatonic Models for Interval Study

(The detailed instructions below and in Unit 2 apply to all eleven units.)

I

Neighboring tone figures outlining tonic triads.

These neighboring tone figures consist of major or minor 2nds that emphasize notes of the tonic triad in major, minor, Mixolydian, Lydian, Phrygian, and Dorian modes. Nevertheless, it is not necessary to have a knowledge of modes or triads in order to complete these exercises.

1. The stemmed notes outline tonic triads.
2. The unstemmed notes form either a major or minor second with the stemmed notes.
3. The slurs indicate the dependence of the unstemmed notes (neighboring tones) on the stemmed notes (notes of the tonic triad).

Procedure

Exercises 1–24

Follow steps 1, 2, and 3 below:

Step 1. The instructor establishes the key of C major for you by playing or singing exercises 1–4 (as shown in the following model):

Step 2. Your instructor now plays or sings the first stemmed note (C).

Step 3. Sing the given note, the major 2nd above, and return using whatever system your instructor requests.

Step 4. Continue steps 1–3 until all neighboring tone figures are completed in **C major.** Then, return to step 1 and repeat the procedure in **A minor** (figures 5a–8a). If your instructor requests, continue with each of the modes: Mixolydian (figures 9a–12a), Lydian (figures 13a–16a), Phrygian (figures 17a–20a), and Dorian (figures 21a–24a). For those who prefer parallel minor, and so on, see figures 5b–24b. (Cautionary accidentals are added to remind students to retain the appropriate key signature for each of the transposed modes.)

In a very short time you will become familiar with the tonic triad for each of the modes, since each of the stemmed notes represents a note of the tonic triad. Once you have completed the first four units of this text, you should return to these familiar diatonic models for practice in clef reading.

II

Neighboring tone figures in combination with passing tone figures outlining a descending line from scale degrees 5 to 1. Exercises 25–26 combine neighboring and passing tone figures to fill in a descending line from scale degrees 5 to 1 in major and minor. These passages (or *vocalises*) may be used for tonal exercises and melodies throughout the book, as a way of establishing the key.

Procedure

Exercises 25–26

Step 1. Your instructor sings or plays figure 25b (major) as a means of establishing the key.
Step 2. Repeat (sing) the same figure your instructor provides in step 1.
Step 3. For additional practice, follow the same procedure in each major key by moving down a perfect fifth (or up a perfect fourth), first to F major, then to Bb, Eb, and so on. Please see the following model:

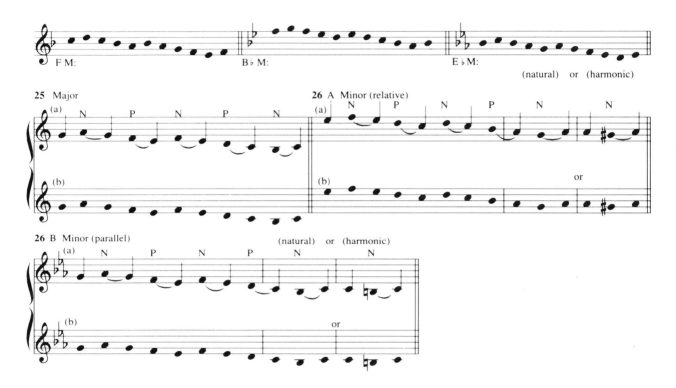

D. SS Melodic Fragments for Interval Singing

These melodic fragments are taken from music literature for the purpose of providing a musical context for the intervals (M2nd and m2nd) introduced in Section C. Examples of neighboring and passing tones occur in abundance.

Procedure

1. Your instructor establishes the key for each of the fragments, using one of the *vocalises* taught in exercises 25 and 26 transposed to the appropriate pitch level.
2. Sing the following excerpts and identify neighboring and passing tone figures, as well as intervals.

1 Lord Have Mercy – Requiem Mass. Gregorian Chant

2 Come Holy Spirit – Pentecost (abridged). Gregorian Chant

3 Praise – Passover. Adapted from Songs of the Babylonian Jews

4 Forgiveness (a specific series of blessings). Adapted from Songs of the Babylonian Jews

E. ET Models and Embellishments: Short Melodic Structures

1. Before coming to class, play and sing the melodic structures in the models. Your instructor will review those structures at the beginning of this lesson.
2. Your instructor will play the given musical structure followed by embellishments of that structure. Notice how notes and rhythms are added to the melodic structure.
3. Memorize the sound of each melody and repeat its sound in your mind. Write the notes of the melody on the numbered staves provided below each model.
4. As you proceed through the lesson, the embellishments will be more elaborate. Keep the structure in mind as you listen to each embellished melody. Try to hear that structure "through" the embellishments.

Model:

Embellishments:

1

2

F. SS Melodies: M2, m2

Procedure for Completing Each Melody

1. First, sing the scale upon which the melody is constructed. Use syllables or numbers as suggested by your instructor.
2. When you are familiar with the scale, then sing each melody using the same syllables or numbers.
3. Circle the 1st, 3rd, and 5th scale degrees as reference tones if you encounter difficulty.
4. Remember that you learn *only* when you sing the correct pitch and syllable or number. So, do not hesitate to repeat a melody until you are satisfied that you have sung it correctly.
5. Tempo is important. Sing each melody slowly at first. If you can increase the tempo without making mistakes, do so.

1 Scale: C Major ♩ – 76

2 Scale: G Major

3 Scale: F Major ♩ – 76

4 Scale: D Major ♪ – 96

5 Scale: B-flat Major ♩ — 76

6 Scale: A Major ♩ – 76

7 Scale: E-flat Major ♪ — 76

14   Andante
Scale: B-flat Major

15   Moderato
Scale: D Major

The last four measures of number 16 are in contrary motion to the first four.

16   Allegretto
Scale: E-flat Major

17   Andante con moto
Scale: A Major

18 Presto
Scale: A-flat Major

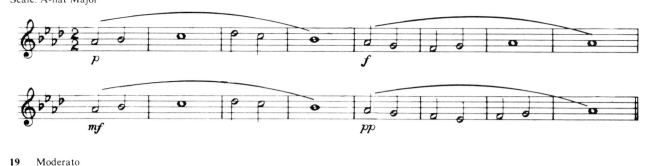

19 Moderato
Scale: E Major

20 Allegro
Scale: C Major

G. ET Melodic Dictation: Scalewise
(Conjunct Diatonic) Melodies

Each exercise consists of a short melodic phrase. Listen to the phrase as it is played. Complete the phrase on the staff in notation.

1. As you listen to each melody the first time, try to memorize it immediately—in its entirety.
2. Do *not* write anything on paper yet! You will learn almost nothing by trying to write too early.
3. Sing as much of the melody as you can from the first hearing before you listen to it again.
4. Continue to listen until you can hear all the pitches. Do it in three hearings if you can. Sing the entire melody from memory.
5. Only after you have the entire melody memorized should you attempt to write anything on paper!
6. Observe that when you have the melody memorized, you can slow it down sufficiently to write the notes on the staff as you sing (or preferably think).
7. Write the melody on the staff in music notation.

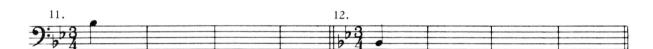

H. SS Melodies (Major): P5, P4, M3, m3
Within the Tonic Triad, and M2, m2

Procedure for Singing Each Exercise

1. First sing the scale related to each exercise—as usual using syllables or numbers.
2. Then, sing each exercise with the same syllables or numbers.
3. For the present, do not worry about the intervals formed by scale steps 1, 3, and 5. Think of these primarily as *reference tones*—tones to be memorized.

I. ET Intervals: m2, M2, m3, M3

Each exercise consists of a single interval.

1. You can use your knowledge of the major and harmonic minor scale in recognizing intervals. Think of the intervals in this section as pitches of a major or harmonic scale:

   minor 2nd (m2) = sounds like the leading tone to tonic (scale degrees 7 to 8 or ti to do) of a major scale

   Major 2nd (M2) = sounds like the tonic to supertonic (scale degrees 1 to 2 or do to re) in the major scale

   minor 3rd (m3) = sounds like the tonic to mediant (scale degrees 1 to 3 or la to do) in the minor scale

   Major 3rd (M3) = sounds like the tonic to mediant (scale degrees 1 to 3 or do to mi) in the major scale

2. When you have related the sound of an interval to pitches found in the major or harmonic minor scale, then you are ready to write the answer.
3. Write the missing note of the interval on the staff.
4. Write the name of the interval in the space provided.

The given note is the lower of the two:

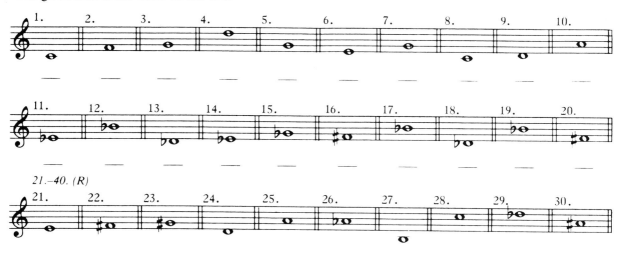

21.–40. (R)

The given note is the upper of the two:

J. SS Ensemble Excerpts—Two Voices: M2, m2

Procedure

1. This two-voice section is intended to provide practice in *ensemble* singing. These melodies are similar to those found in Section F of this unit, but you must now learn to cope with another voice that will be singing different pitches.
2. Your instructor will select either two individuals or two sections of the class to sing these phrases.
3. Follow the directions found in Section F of this unit.
4. Learn to create a good ensemble sound with the other simultaneous voice, but at the same time do not allow it to distract or interfere with your own concentration. Ensemble performance is an art in its own right and well worth learning!

K. ET Chord Identification: Major and Minor Triads

Each exercise consists of a single triad. Recognize the quality of these major and minor triads.

1. For numbers 1–20 (triads in simple position):
   1. Write large M for major or small m for minor in the blanks provided.
   2. If your instructor requests it, also write the triad on the staff. The *roots* of the triads are given.
2. For numbers 21–40 (triads in four voices—a few inversions):
   1. Circle either large M or small m indicating the sound of the triad played.
   2. Your instructor may ask you to spell the triad orally in class.

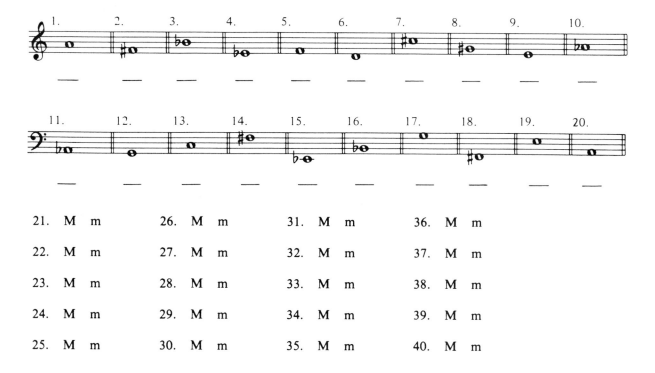

21. M m	26. M m	31. M m	36. M m
22. M m	27. M m	32. M m	37. M m
23. M m	28. M m	33. M m	38. M m
24. M m	29. M m	34. M m	39. M m
25. M m	30. M m	35. M m	40. M m

L. ET Harmonic Function: I and V Triads

Each exercise consists of four triads in four-voice harmony.

1. Make sure you can hear the bass note of four-voice triads in root position. Outside of class play the following triads and try to match the pitches of the bass notes by singing them in your own voice range.

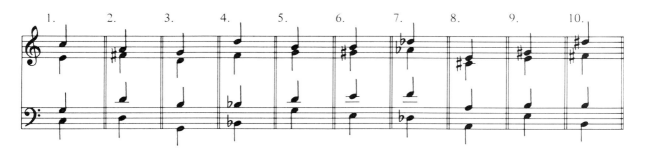

2. Listen to the four triads in each of these exercises. All are in the key of C major. Make sure you have the tonic pitch (C) well in mind.
3. All triads in numbers 1–15 are in root position. Isolate and identify the scale degree (number or syllables) of each base note by singing it.
4. Write the analysis of the four triads in the blanks by changing the scale numbers or syllables to roman numerals.

Scale Number		Syllable		Roman Numeral
1	or	do	=	I
5	or	sol	=	V

1.–10. (R)

1. _____ _____ _____ _____   9. _____ _____ _____ _____

2. _____ _____ _____ _____   10. _____ _____ _____ _____

3. _____ _____ _____ _____   11. _____ _____ _____ _____

4. _____ _____ _____ _____   12. _____ _____ _____ _____

5. _____ _____ _____ _____   13. _____ _____ _____ _____

6. _____ _____ _____ _____   14. _____ _____ _____ _____

7. _____ _____ _____ _____   15. _____ _____ _____ _____

8. _____ _____ _____ _____

Numbers 16–25 contain **triad inversions**—the root is not the lowest note. The exercises in Unit 4, Section K will help you to identify inversions. Practice them with tapes, or play chords in inversions before you listen to numbers 16–25.

16. _____ _____ _____ _____   21. _____ _____ _____ _____

17. _____ _____ _____ _____   22. _____ _____ _____ _____

18. _____ _____ _____ _____   23. _____ _____ _____ _____

19. _____ _____ _____ _____   24. _____ _____ _____ _____

20. _____ _____ _____ _____   25. _____ _____ _____ _____

2

A. SS Rhythm: Practicing Compound Meter

I

Consider each measure as a module to be sung separately or as part of a series.

1. Say rhythm for each measure separately, repeating it several times—until you can achieve at least a moderate tempo.
2. If your instructor recommends, conduct yourself using the hand movements illustrated in Unit 1, page 2.
3. When each measure is well within your grasp, try an entire line, performing all modules one after the other.
4. Accuracy is the prime goal. Speed (fast tempo) is desirable, but not absolutely essential at the moment.
5. If measures 29–40 are too difficult for the moment, omit them and return later.

Rhythm Syllables

Select one of the two systems below:

1	1 an du 2 an du	1 du 2 du 1 2 le
2	1 la le 2 la le	1 le 2 le 1 2 le

Pronunciation:

AN as in *ANOTHER*
DU as in *DUMP*
LA as in *LARVA*
LE as in *LEE*

After completing these rhythm exercises as suggested at the beginning of the section, ask half the class to clap or say a line forward while the other half reads the same line backward from end to beginning. To create a different quality of sound for each section, have the second group drum on their chairs with the palms of their hands.

II

Sing the following exercises on a neutral pitch.

1. Clap the meter.
   Say the rhythm using rhythm syllables.
2. Say the meter using numbers.
   Clap the rhythm.

3. Tap the meter with one hand.
   Tap the rhythm with the other hand.
4. Half the class taps the meter.
   The other half taps the rhythm.

Rhythm syllables:

7   Rhythmic alternation (examples also of rhythmic hocket)

8   Rhythmic Imitation

9   Rhythmic Imitation

B. ET Rhythmic Dictation: Duple and Triple Subdivisions of the Beat

Each exercise consists of a three-measure melody. Complete the rhythm (only) of each exercise on the lines provided.

1. As you hear the preparatory measure(s), count the meter. If the meter is 3/4, count 1–2–3.
2. After the first hearing: Say or clap the rhythm immediately.
3. After the second hearing: Count the meter beats and clap rhythm immediately. When you are sure of the rhythm, write it on the appropriate line.
4. If a third hearing is needed: Use it to verify rhythms you have written down or to clear up any misconceptions.

Listen to the rhythm as many times as you require to get the right answer. Accuracy is the most important item for the moment.

The following example indicates the correct procedure.

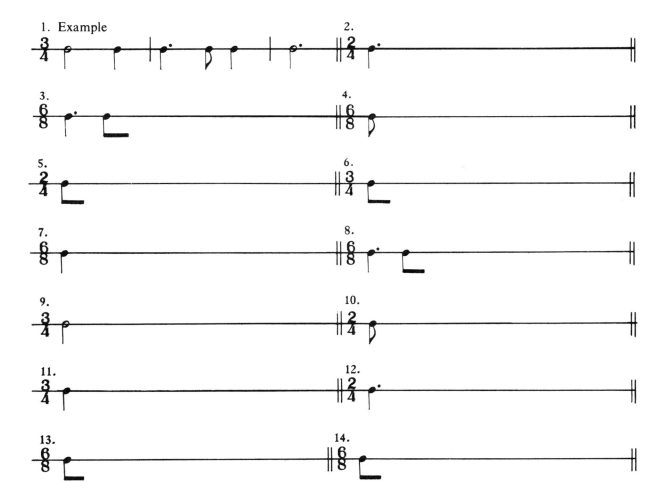

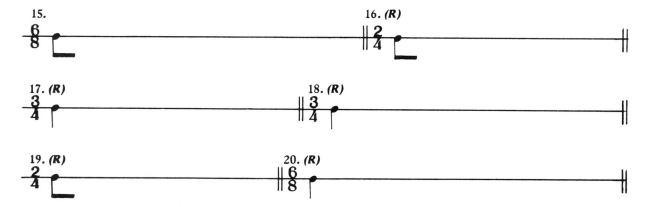

C. SS Diatonic Models for Interval Study
New Intervals: P5, P4, M3, m3
Review: M2, m2

(The detailed instructions below apply to all eleven units.)

I

Passing tone figures in major filling in thirds.

Procedure

Exercises 1–8

Step 1. Your instructor establishes the key of G major by playing or singing the *vocalise* in G major:

Step 2. Your instructor plays or sings the first stemmed note G (no. 1 of the following eight exercises). Sing the given note and two major 2nds (M2) in ascending motion. In the next exercise (no. 2), your instructor plays or sings the first stemmed note (B) and asks you to sing the given note and two major 2nds (M2) in descending motion. In exercise no. 3, repeat the procedure for exercise no. 1.

Step 3. For additional practice, your instructor plays or sings the first stemmed note of each exercise and asks class members to take turns singing all eight exercises.

Step 4. Using another approach, sing the entire set of eight exercises first in the given key (G), then in C, F, B♭, and so on. Please see the following model:

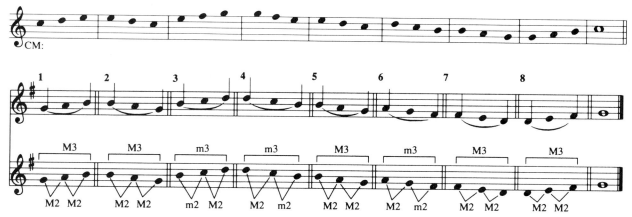

II

Intervals of the third outlining perfect fifths in major keys.

Procedure

Exercises 9–16

Step 1. Same as Step 1 above.

Step 2. Your instructor plays or sings the first note (G) of no. 9 (exercises below), and you respond by singing the given note and a major third above.

In no. 10, the instructor plays or sings the first note (B) and asks you to sing the given note and a major third below. Continue this same procedure through no. 16.

Step 3. As above, class members sing the exercises in turn.

Step 4. As above, sing the entire set from nos. 9–16 not only in G major, but in the keys of C, F, B♭, and so on.

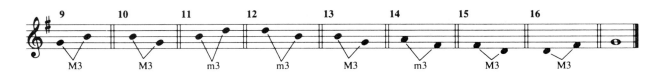

Exercises 17–20

Step 1. Your instructor plays the first note (G) of no. 17 and asks you to sing all three notes.
Continue in the same manner with nos. 18 and 19.

Step 2. Nos. 17 and 18 outline the tonic triad, no. 19 the dominant, and no. 20 brings you back to the tonic.
Sing the set of exercises from 17–20, and your instructor will point out the tonic and dominant.

Step 3. Sing nos. 17–20 as written (in G major), then transpose the entire set down a perfect fifth to the key of C major. Continue the process through the keys of F, B♭, E♭, and so on.

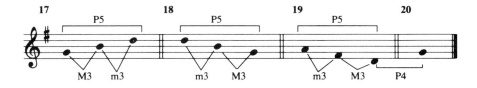

Exercises 21–24

These exercises outline the triads found in nos. 17–20. Using the same steps (exercises 17–20) complete nos. 21–24, and sing them in various keys as shown in Step 3 above.

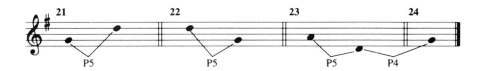

III

Passing tone figures in minor filling in thirds. The four passing tone figures (exercises 25–28) anticipate melodic fragment 2 (see Section D, page 32) from the Bach chorale no. 48, *Ach wie nichtig, ach wie flüchtig,* and consist of one major second (M2) and one minor second (m2), filling in a minor third.

Procedure

Exercises 25a–28a

Follow the same procedure for passing tone figures in major keys (page 28). Use the minor *vocalise* in E minor (relative minor). (For exercises in parallel minor (G minor) see exercises 26b–36b.):

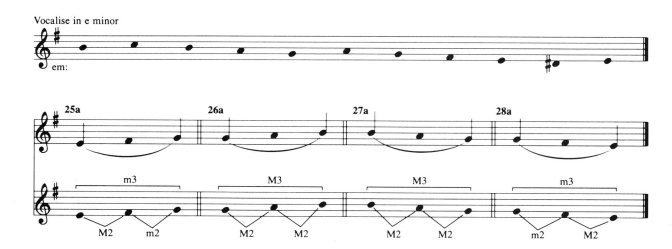

IV

Intervals of the third outlining perfect fifths in minor.
In the previous passing tone exercises (25–28) the stemmed notes formed thirds, which in turn outlined triads.
Exercises 29–32 contain the notes that were stemmed in exercises 25–28, thus representing a melodic reduction of figures 25–28.

Procedure

Exercises 29a–36a

Use the same procedures described for exercises 25–28 (above).

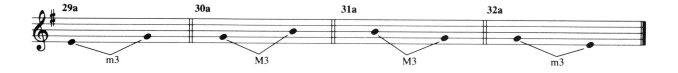

Exercises 33 and 34 are reductions of exercises 29–32.

Exercises 35 and 36 are reductions of exercises 33–34.

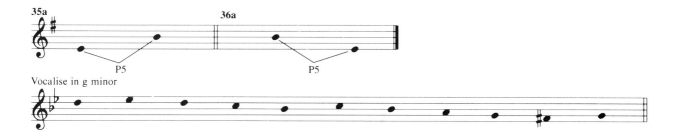

Vocalise in g minor

Exercises 25b–36b

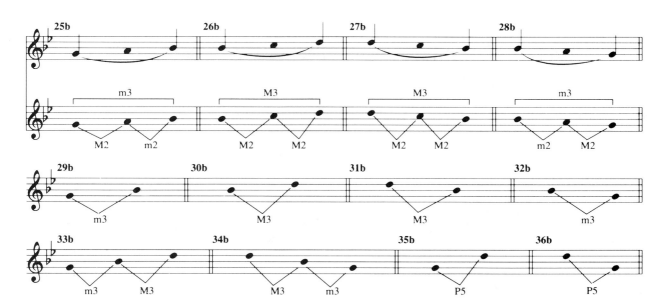

V

Intervals of the P4, P5, and M3 supporting a melodic stepwise ascent from scale degrees 1 to 3. Exercises 37–40 anticipate melodic fragment no. 3 (Section D, page 32) from the Mozart *Requiem*.

Procedure

Exercises 37–40

Follow the same procedure as before. Your instructor establishes the key with the *vocalise* in G major, playing the stemmed notes, and you sing all pitches. After completing the exercises, sing the entire pattern in different keys as illustrated in the following model:

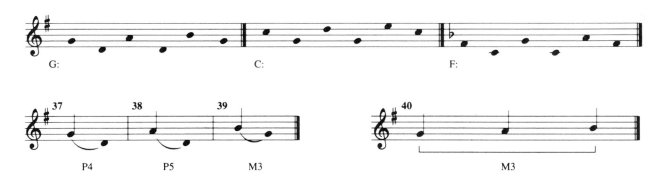

D. SS Melodic Fragments for Interval Singing:
P5, P4, M3, m3, M2, m2

These melodic fragments are taken from music literature for the purpose of providing a musical context for the intervals introduced in Section C.

Follow the procedure outlined in Unit I, Section D.

E. ET Models and Embellishments: Short Melodic Structures

1. Before coming to class, play and sing the melodic structures in the models. Your instructor will review those structures at the beginning of this lesson.
2. Your instructor will play the given musical structure followed by embellishments of that structure. Notice how notes and rhythms are added to the melodic structure.
3. Memorize the sound of each melody and repeat its sound in your mind. Write the notes of the melody on the numbered staves provided below model B.
4. As you proceed through the lesson, the embellishments will be more elaborate. Keep the structure in mind as you listen to each embellished melody. Try to hear that structure "through" the embellishments.

One additional example based on this model and Unit 1 E. See G. F. Handel: The Messiah, "And he shall purify."

F. SS Melodies: P5, P4, M3, m3 Within the Tonic Triad, and M2, m2, P8

The melodic content of this section focuses on some leaps within the tonic triad (M3, m3, P5, P4) as well as stepwise motion (M2, m2) in C major.

While valuable for review and practice in singing at performance tempo, these drills are also suitable for developing the art of clef reading as a means of transposing from one key to another. For example, the same phrase is used in both no. 1 and 11, except that in no. 11 the alto clef is introduced. This places middle C (c') on the middle line. The alto clef in no. 11 makes it possible to transpose no. 1 to the key of D major without changing the position of any of the notes on the staff.

Procedure

1. In your mind, replace the **treble** clef in no. 2 with an **alto** clef (see no. 11 to visualize an alto clef).
2. Since all melodies in this chapter are in C major, you know that no. 2 begins on the dominant (5 or sol).
3. When you visualize no. 2 with an alto clef, the first pitch is A (below middle C). A is now the dominant, so D is the tonic of the melody.
4. Imagine two sharps (F♯ and C♯) in the signature, and sing the melody in the same manner as you sing it in C major with a treble clef.
5. If you sing the melody in alto clef, it will be a seventh lower than in treble, but most melodies in this book are intended to be sung in whatever range the singer finds most comfortable.
6. If you have trouble reading in the alto clef, check your accuracy by going back to C major with a treble clef and singing the melody again.
7. You unfamiliarity with this new clef will disappear presently, and you will have learned a valuable new skill that you may use many times later on.

G. ET Scales: Major Scale and Three Forms of the Minor Scale

For each exercise write the type of scale you hear.

Exercises 1–10	consist of a major, natural minor, harmonic minor, or melodic minor scale.
Exercises 11–20	consist of short melodic excerpts from music literature based on one of these scales.
Natural minor	follows the key signature

Harmonic minor	key signature plus raised 7th scale degree.

Ascending melodic minor	key signature plus raised 6th and 7th scale degrees.

Major   follows the key signature.

Write the name of the scale in the blank provided.   *11.–20. (R)*

1. _____   11. _____

2. _____   12. _____

3. _____   13. _____

4. _____   14. _____

5. _____   15. _____

6. _____   16. _____

7. _____   17. _____

8. _____   18. _____

9. _____   19. _____

10. _____   20. _____

H. SS Melodies (Major): P5, P4, M3, m3
Within the Tonic Triad, and M2, m2

I

The following melodies excerpted from music literature illustrate the same intervals presented in Section F of this unit.

Numbers 1–10 are from Beethoven's symphonic works, and 11–20 are from Haydn's keyboard compositions. For the purposes of this unit, some melodies have been slightly altered or abridged. The authors of this book adjusted the melodies in order to insure a comfortable singing range and to stay within the limitations imposed by the materials of the first two units (i.e., M2, m2, M3, m3, P5, P4).

Sing these melodies using whatever procedures your instructor requests.

II

The following are adapted Amish songs and hymn tunes.

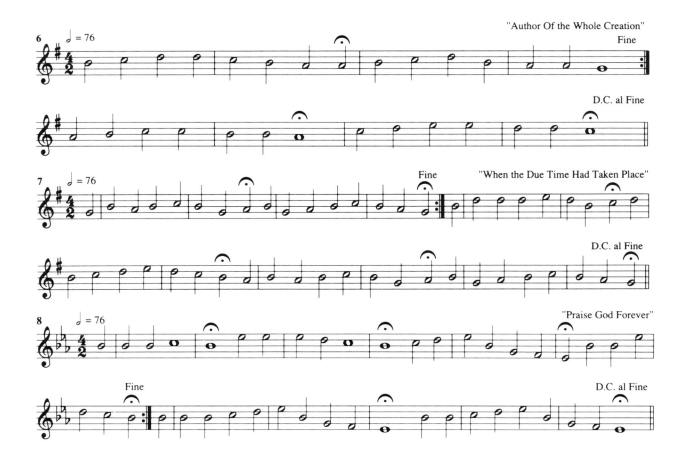

I. ET Scale Degrees: Single Notes

First you will hear a C major scale, followed by one of the pitches of that scale. Write the number (1 to 7) or syllable (do to ti) of the one pitch played.

1. Sing the scale (using numbers or syllables) until it is familiar to you.
2. If you have difficulty remembering the pitch of *all* scale degrees, be sure to remember at least 1 and 5 (do and sol). These two can be used as reference tones—landmarks that will help to locate other scale degrees.
3. When you hear the single pitch (after the scale is played), sing (or *think*) it immediately.
4. Then, relate it to one of the reference tones, tonic (first scale step) or dominant (fifth scale step)— whichever is closest, and sing stepwise to that reference tone.

5. You will know the identity of the pitch played by the number of scale steps you sang to get to the reference tone.
6. When you are sure of your answer, write it in the appropriate blank.

1. _____   11. _____
2. _____   12. _____
3. _____   13. _____
4. _____   14. _____
5. _____   15. _____
6. _____   16. _____
7. _____   17. _____
8. _____   18. _____
9. _____   19. _____
10. _____   20. _____

J. SS Ensemble Excerpts—Two Voices:
P5, P4, M3, m3 Within the Tonic Triad, and M2, m2

The ensemble excerpts are from Beethoven's *Missa Solemnis* op. 123. Each melodic line operates within the same intervallic restrictions of Sections F and H of this unit.

Since each excerpt is imitative, sing each line as a separate melodic exercise before you try to put the two together. The texts from the *Gloria, Credo,* and *Sanctus* are provided, although it is not necessary to use words in performance.

1 Allegro vivace   Beethoven   *Missa Solemnis, op. 123, Gloria* (adapted and transposed)

2 Allegro molto   Beethoven   *Missa Solemnis*, op. 123, *Credo* (adapted and transposed)

et a - scen - - - dit in coe - lum

Et a scen - - - dit in coe - - - lum

3 Andante molto cantabile e non troppo mosso   Beethoven   *Missa Solemnis*, op. 123, *Sanctus* (abridged)

Be - ne - di - - ctus Qui ve - nit

Be - ne - di - - ctus Qui ve - nit

in ____ no - mi - ne, no - mi - ne Do - - - mi - ni

in no - mi - ne Do - - mi - ni

K. ET Chord Identification: Major, Minor, and Diminished Triads

Each exercise consists of a single triad. Recognize the quality of each major, minor, or diminished triad.

1. For numbers 1–10 (triads in simple position):
   1. Write large M for major, small m for minor, and small d for diminished triads in the blanks provided.
   2. If your instructor requests it, also write the triad on the staff. The *roots* of the triads are given.
2. For numbers 11–30 (triads in four voices—a few inversions):
   1. Write large M, small m, or small d in the blanks provided.
   2. Your instructor may ask you to spell the triad orally in class.

*See section A of this unit for compound meter.

As a warm-up for ensemble singing, each line should be performed as a solo exercise.

When the students are ready to sing in ensemble, the instructor should provide the first few notes of each part at entrances, either by singing with the students, or by articulating these patterns at the keyboard.

11. _____   21. _____

12. _____   22. _____

13. _____   23. _____

14. _____   24. _____

15. _____   25. _____

16. _____   26. _____

17. _____   27. _____

18. _____   28. _____

19. _____   29. _____

20. _____   30. _____

L. ET Harmonic Function: I, IV, and V Triads

Each exercise consists of four chords in four-part block harmony. Write the roman-numeral analysis of each chord in the blanks provided.

A list of suggested strategies for this section can be found in Unit 1, Section L.

When this section is assigned to students, refer them to Unit 1, Section L for review. A rehearsal of the entire procedure is helpful.

Numbers 1–15 consist of the following root-position triads only:

A M: I   IV   V

1.–10. (R)

1. _____

2. _____

3. _____

4. _____

5. _____

6. _____

7. _____

8. _____

9. _____

10. _____

11. _____

12. _____

13. _____

14. _____

15. _____

Numbers 16–25 contain at least one inversion:

16. _____

17. _____

18. _____

19. _____

20. _____

21. _____

22. _____

23. _____

24. _____

25. _____

• • • • • • 3 • • • • • •

A. SS Rhythm: Concentration on Half-Beat Values

I

Consider each measure as a module to be sung separately or as part of a series.

1. Follow the procedures given in Unit 2, Section A, page 23.
2. If your instructor recommends, conduct yourself using the hand movements illustrated in Unit 1, page 2.
3. Accuracy is the prime goal. Speed (fast tempo) is desirable, but not absolutely essential at the moment.
4. If any of the measures are too difficult for the moment, omit them and return later.

Rhythm syllables:

Used by some: 1 and 2 and 3 and 4 and
Used by others: 1 te 2 te 3 te 4 te

Examples:

1

II

Sing the following exercises on a neutral pitch.

1. Clap the meter.
   Say the rhythm using rhythm syllables.
2. Say the meter using numbers.
   Clap the rhythm.
3. Tap the meter with one hand and the rhythm with the other hand.

Sing these two-voice rhythm exercises in the following ways:

1. One student recites the rhythm of the upper line while another recites the rhythm of the lower line.
2. One student recites the rhythm of the upper line while clapping the rhythm of the lower line.
3. One student taps the rhythm of the upper line with one hand and the rhythm of the lower line with the other hand.

9 Rhythmic Canon

10 Some Rhythmic Imitation

B. ET Rhythmic Dictation: Full-Beat and Half-Beat Values

Most exercises consist of two measures in 2/4, 3/4, or 4/4 meter.

1. For numbers 1–10, the meter signature and first-note value(s) are given.
2. For numbers 11–20, nothing is given, but the instructor will provide the basic beat before beginning the exercise.
3. For helpful suggestions, see Unit 1, Section B.
4. Complete the rhythm using a neutral pitch.

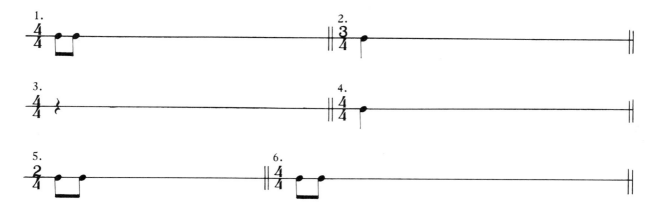

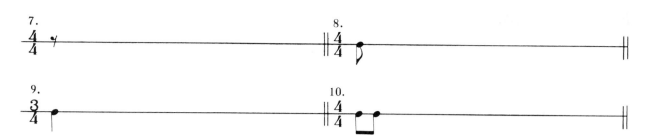

5. Write the meter signature and the rhythm using a neutral pitch. The instructor will provide the meter beat before beginning each exercise.

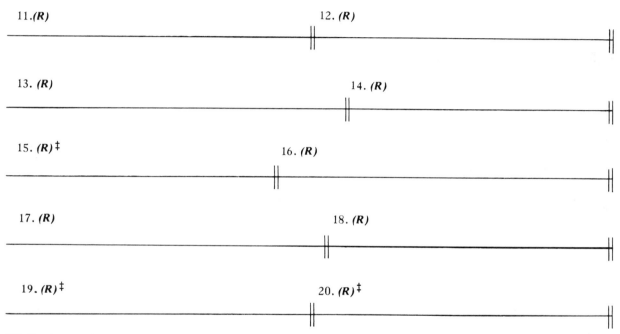

11.*(R)*   12. *(R)*

13. *(R)*   14. *(R)*

15. *(R)* ‡   16. *(R)*

17. *(R)*   18. *(R)*

19. *(R)* ‡   20. *(R)* ‡

‡Challenging exercise

C. SS Diatonic Models for Interval Study
New Interval: P8
Review: P5, P4, M3, m3, M2, m2

I

Intervals outlining tonic triad and dominant seventh chord.

Exercises 1–10

Follow procedures indicated in Section C of Units 1 and 2 (pages 6 and 28).
For extra practice, use exercises 9 and 10 in each of the major keys, moving down by fourths or up by fifths.
Please see the following model:

Exercises 11–22

Exercises 11–20 outline a theme from the third movement of Haydn's Symphony no. 94. Follow the same procedures as above. For extra practice, sing exercises 21–22 in each of the major keys, moving down by fourths or up by fifths. Please see the following model:

II

Intervals emphasizing the tonic triad in minor, with special emphasis on the perfect fourth.

Exercises 23–28

Exercises 23–26 outline a theme adapted from a set of Mozart Variations, KV 573, in anticipation of the melodic fragment in Section D (page 52).

Follow the same procedures as above. For extra practice, sing exercises 27–28 in minor keys, moving down by fifths or up by fourths. Please see the following model:

Exercises 29–35

Exercises 29–33 outline a theme adapted from a Mozart Minuet, KV 315g, in anticipation of melodic fragment no. 4 in Section D (following).

Follow the same procedures as above. Sing exercises 34–35 in each of the minor keys as shown in the following model:

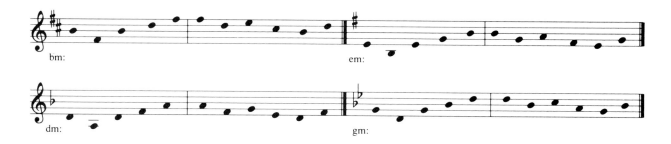

D. SS Melodic Fragments for Interval Singing
New Interval: P8
Review: P5, P4, M3, m3, M2, m2

Sing the following excerpts using correct note values and pitches.

(Note to the instructor: Relate the following melodies to exercises in Section C [pages 50–52].)

Exercises:

E. ET Models and Embellishments:
Simple Melodic Structures

1. Play and sing the melodic structure in the model before coming to class. Your instructor will review those structures at the beginning of this lesson.
2. Your instructor will play the given musical structure followed by embellishments of that structure.
3. Write the model's embellishments on the numbered staves provided.

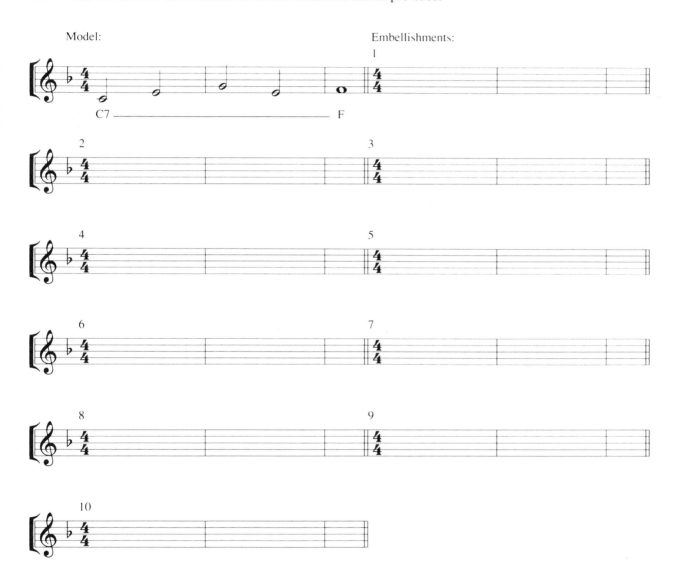

F. SS Melodies (Major): P5, P4, M3, m3
Within the Tonic Triad, and M2, m2

Procedure for Completing Each Melody

1. First, sing the scale upon which the melody is constructed. Use syllables or numbers as suggested by your instructor.
2. When you are familiar with the scale, sing each melody using the same syllables or numbers.
3. Circle the 1st, 3rd, and 5th scale degrees as reference tones if you encounter difficulty.
4. Remember that you learn *only* when you sing the correct pitch and syllable or number. So, do not hesitate to repeat a melody until you are satisfied that you have sung it correctly.
5. Tempo is important. Sing each melody slowly at first. If you can increase the tempo without making mistakes, do so.

G. ET Melodic Dictation: Dictation Employing m2, M2, m3, M3

Each exercise consists of a short melody.

1. Memorize the melody before trying to write it down.
2. If your instructor requests, sing the entire melody using solfeggio syllables (do re mi) or numbers (1, 2, 3, etc.).
3. When you know the melody thoroughly, write it on the appropriate staff.

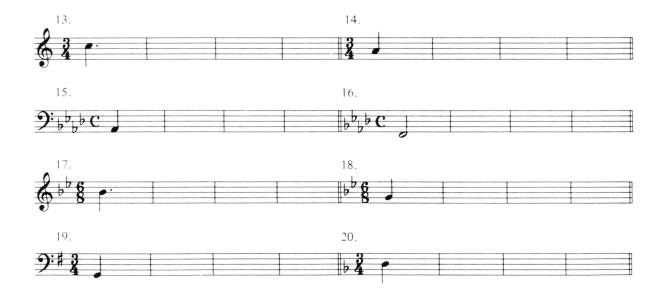

*(R) means recorded.

H. SS Melodies (Minor)

I: P5, P4, M3, m3 within the Tonic Triad

1. First sing the scale related to each exercise—as usual, with syllables or numbers.
2. Then, sing each melody with the same syllables or numbers.
3. For the moment, do not worry about the intervals formed by scale steps 1, 3, and 5. Think of these primarily as *reference tones*—tones from which other scale degrees may be located.

4

5

II: Natural, Harmonic, and Melodic Minor

The first example shows a single melody repeated to illustrate the three forms of the minor scale. Sing all three forms, one after the other, and note the effect created by each. Examples 2, 3, and 4 are in natural minor.

1 A Natural Minor

B Harmonic Minor

C Melodic Minor

2

3

4

III: P5, P4, M3, m3 Within the Tonic Triad

Follow procedures outlined in Unit 2, Section F.

IV: Transposition and Inversion

The first three examples of Gregorian chant are modal in character and are transcribed in modern notation. If sung as printed, these melodies will afford a valuable opportunity to get acquainted with music written before the advent of the major/minor system.

For some additional practice in clef reading and transposition:

1. Transpose no. 1 (*Kyrie XI—Orbis factor*). When you visualize the alto clef, think of the melody as being in E minor (Aeolian mode), so include F♯ in the signature.
2. Transpose no. 2 (*Sanctus IX—Cum jubilo*). This was originally considered to be in the Ionian mode (now our major mode). When you visualize the alto clef, also add an F♯ to the key signature. The starting note is d′.
3. Melodies 3 and 4 are closely related. The *Kyrie IX* (Cum jubilo) (no. 3) is the source for Josquin's *Missa de Beata Virgine* (no. 4). The alto voice is shown here. When you visualize the alto clef, see if you can figure out the correct signatures.
4. Melodies 5 and 6 are from Contrapunctus XII of Bach's *Art of the Fugue*. No. 6 is the melodic inversion of no. 5.

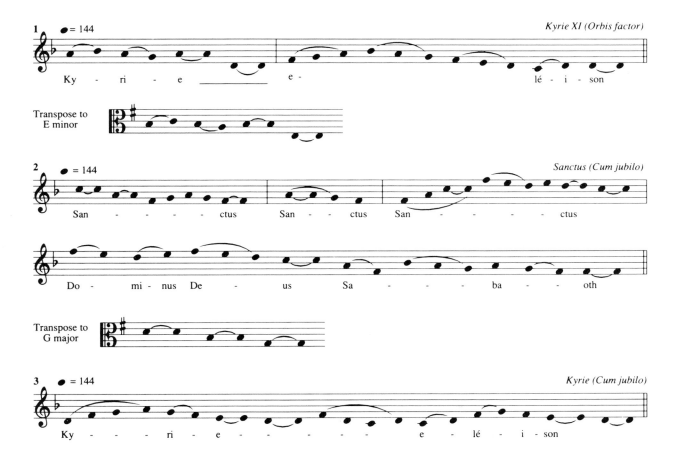

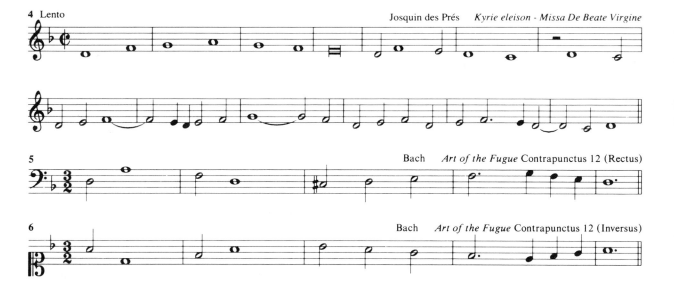

4 Lento

Josquin des Prés · *Kyrie eleison - Missa De Beate Virgine*

5

Bach · *Art of the Fugue* Contrapunctus 12 (Rectus)

6

Bach · *Art of the Fugue* Contrapunctus 12 (Inversus)

I. ET New Intervals: P5 and P4

Each exercise consists of a single interval. The first note is given.

1. Write the second note of the interval on the staff.
2. Place the name of the interval (P4, m2, M3, and so on) in the blank provided.
3. To help you recognize intervals, think of them as parts of a scale:

   P5 = tonic to 5th of a major or minor scale

   P4 = tonic to 4th scale degree of a major or minor scale

   M3 = tonic to 3rd of a major scale

   m3 = tonic to 3rd of a minor scale

   M2 = tonic to 2nd degree of a major or minor scale

   m2 = leading tone to tonic of a major or harmonic minor scale

The second note is above the given tone:

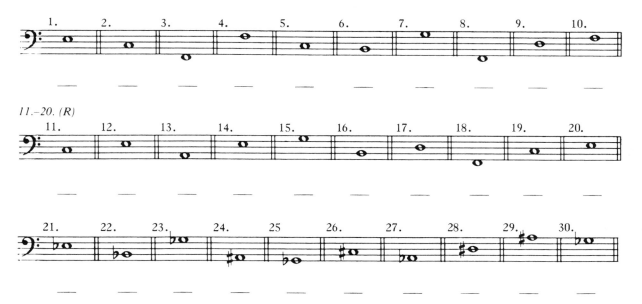

11.–20. (R)

The second note is below the given tone:

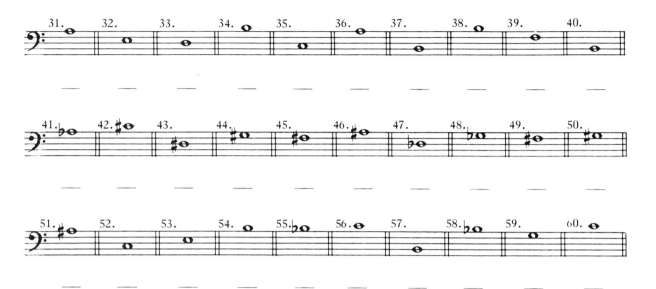

J. SS Ensemble Excerpts—Two Voices:
P5, P4, M3, m3 Within the Tonic Triad

Procedure

1. This two-voice section is intended to provide practice in *ensemble* singing. These melodies are similar to those found in Section F of this chapter, but you must now learn to cope with another voice that will be singing different pitches.
2. Your instructor will select either two individuals or two sections of the class to sing these phrases.
3. Follow the directions found in Section F of this chapter.
4. Learn to create a good ensemble sound with the other simultaneous voice, but at the same time do not allow it to distract or interfere with your own concentration. Ensemble performance is an art in its own right and well worth learning!

K. ET Chord Identification:
Triad Factors in the Soprano

Each exercise consists of a single chord. Write the number of the chord factor (1, 3, 5) in the soprano voice.

Suggestions:

1. First, you will hear a triad in simple (closest possible) position. Sing it—1–3–5–3–1.
2. Then, the same triad will be played in four-part harmony. Remember that the root will be the bass note, but aside from that the chord tones in the tenor, alto, or soprano voices may be in any order.

3. After the four-voice triad is played, the soprano note will be repeated alone. Sing or *think* it immediately! Keep its pitch in your mind.
4. Recollect the sound of the simple triad first heard (number 1) and determine whether the soprano pitch is the root, 3rd, or 5th.
5. When you are convinced, write 1, 3, or 5 in the blank provided.

Write the number (1, 3, or 5) of the chord factor in the soprano.

13.–24. (R)

1. _____   7. _____   13. _____   19. _____

2. _____   8. _____   14. _____   20. _____

3. _____   9. _____   15. _____   21. _____

4. _____   10. _____   16. _____   22. _____

5. _____   11. _____   17. _____   23. _____

6. _____   12. _____   18. _____   24. _____

L. ET Harmonic Function: I, ii, and V Triads

Each exercise consists of four triads in four-voice harmony.

1. Make sure you can hear the bass note of four-voice triads in root position. Outside of class play the following triads and try to match the pitches of the bass notes by singing them in your own voice range.

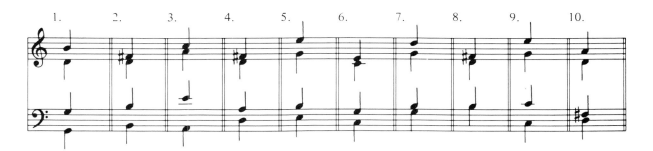

2. Listen to the four triads in each of these exercises. All are in the key of G major. Make sure you have the tonic pitch (G) well in mind.
3. All triads in numbers 1–15 are in root position. Isolate and identify the scale degree (number or syllable) of each bass note by singing it.
4. Write the analysis of the four triads in the blanks by changing the numbers or syllables to roman numerals.

Numbers 1–15 contain root-position triads only:

8.–15. (R)

1. _____ _____ _____ _____   8. _____ _____ _____ _____

2. _____ _____ _____ _____   9. _____ _____ _____ _____

3. _____ _____ _____ _____   10. _____ _____ _____ _____

4. _____ _____ _____ _____   11. _____ _____ _____ _____

5. _____ _____ _____ _____   12. _____ _____ _____ _____

6. _____ _____ _____ _____   13. _____ _____ _____ _____

7. _____ _____ _____ _____   14. _____ _____ _____ _____

                                                15. _____ _____ _____ _____

Numbers 16–25 contain triad inversions.

16. _____ _____ _____ _____   21. _____ _____ _____ _____

17. _____ _____ _____ _____   22. _____ _____ _____ _____

18. _____ _____ _____ _____   23. _____ _____ _____ _____

19. _____ _____ _____ _____   24. _____ _____ _____ _____

20. _____ _____ _____ _____   25. _____ _____ _____ _____

4

A. SS Rhythm: Concentration on Easier Quarter-Beat Values

I

Consider each measure as a module to be sung separately or as part of a series.

1. Follow procedures given in Unit 2, Section A, page 23.
2. If your instructor recommends, conduct yourself using the hand movements illustrated in Unit 1, page 2.
3. Accuracy is the prime goal. Speed (fast tempo) is desirable, but not absolutely essential at the moment.
4. If any of the measures are too difficult for the moment, omit them and return later.

Rhythm syllables—select either of the two systems:

Some illustrations:

II

Sing the following exercises on a neutral pitch.

1. Clap the meter.
   Say the rhythm using rhythm syllables.
2. Say the meter using numbers.
   Clap the rhythm.
3. Tap the meter with one hand and the rhythm with the other hand.
4. Half the class taps the meter while the other half claps the rhythm.

7 Rhythmic Canon

B. ET Rhythmic Dictation: Half-Beat Values in Syncopation

Each exercise consists of a phrase of music.

Complete the rhythm (neutral pitch) on the staff in notation.

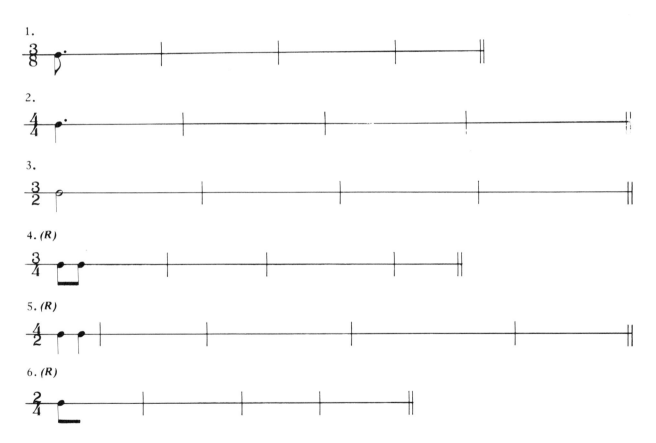

1.

2.

3.

4. *(R)*

5. *(R)*

6. *(R)*

C. SS Diatonic Models for Interval Study
New Interval: m10
Review: P8, P5, P4, M3, m3, M2, m2

I

Intervals outlining tonic triad and dominant seventh chord.

Exercises 1–10

Mozart's "A Little Night Music" provides interesting diatonic models of the tonic and dominant 7th chords. Exercises 1–8 represent an abridgement of the theme that appears in Section D of this chapter (page 70) as the first melodic fragment. Follow the same procedure as in previous chapters. For extra practice, exercises 9–10 may be repeated in all major keys, but by using the last note of the pattern as the first note of the same pattern transposed a fourth lower, or a fifth higher. Please see the following model:

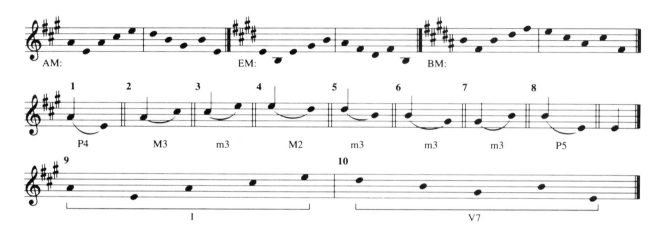

II

Intervals of the P5, P4, M3, m3 filling in an octave.

Exercises 11–17

Exercises 11–15 consist of intervals of the P4th and P5th, filling in an octave. In Section D (page 71), these melodic fragments recur in the Overture to Wagner's "Flying Dutchman" (melody no. 2).

Follow the same procedure as in the previous units. For extra practice, exercises 16–17 can be repeated in all of the minor keys by singing the pattern down a P5th (or up a P4th) through all twelve keys. Please see the following model:

Exercises 18–24

Exercises 18–23 consist of intervals of the P5th, P4th, and M3rd, and m3rd, filling in an octave. In Section D of this chapter (page 71), these melodic figures recur in the excerpt from Schubert's Symphony no. 5, Minuet. Follow the same procedures as in previous units. For extra practice, exercise 24 may be repeated in all minor keys by singing the pattern down a P5th (up a P4th).

III

Intervals of the m10, P4, M3, and m3 outlining the tonic.

Exercises 25–30

The melodic patterns of exercises 25–29 provide an unusual example of a tonic triad, since the interval of a m10th occurs between root and 3rd (exercise 28). These patterns relate to melody no. 4 in Section D of this unit below. Follow the same procedures as in previous units. For extra practice, exercise 30 should be repeated in all minor keys.

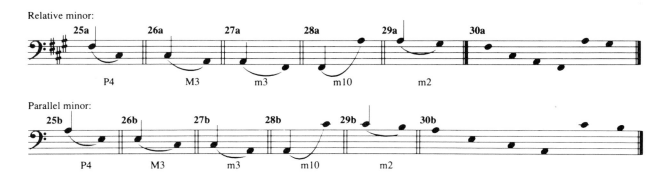

D. SS Melodic Fragments for Interval Singing
New Interval: m10
Review: P8, P5, P4, M3, m3, M2, m2

Sing the following excerpts using correct rhythm and pitch.

(Note to the instructor: Relate the following melodies to exercises in Section C [pages 68–70].)

Exercises:

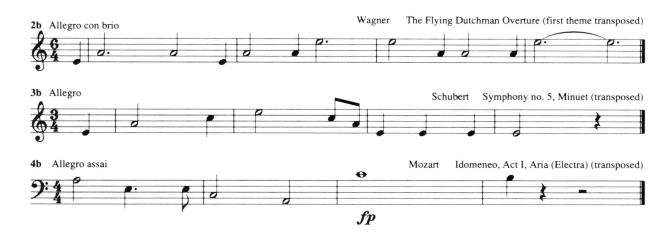

2b Allegro con brio — Wagner — The Flying Dutchman Overture (first theme transposed)

3b Allegro — Schubert — Symphony no. 5, Minuet (transposed)

4b Allegro assai — Mozart — Idomeneo, Act I, Aria (Electra) (transposed)

fp

E. ET Models and Embellishments:
Descending 3rds in Two Voices

1. Notice that the model in this section is a group of descending thirds. This model and its embellishments occur very often in Baroque period music. Listen for these in recordings and concerts. Before coming to class play and sing both parts of the model. Your instructor may choose to review this structure in class.
2. Your instructor will play the structure followed by embellishments of that structure. Notice how the thirds are embellished with additional notes and rhythms in each voice.
3. Memorize the sound of each embellishment and repeat its sound in your mind. Write the model's embellishments on the numbered staves provided.
4. As you proceed through this section, the embellishments will be more elaborate. Keep the structure in mind as you listen to each example. Try to hear that structure "through" the embellishments.

Model:

Embellishments:

1

2

3

F. SS Melodies (Major and Minor):
P5, P4, M3, m3, M2, m2

1. These melodies are limited to the same skips as those in Unit 2, except that the skips may occur between scale tones other than 1–3–5.
2. All melodies except numbers 11–13 are minor.
3. Except for the final four, melodies in this section are excerpted from folk song literature.
4. All rhythms were presented in previous units.
5. Follow directions as printed in Unit 3, section F, page 54.
6. In melodies 1–6 chord symbols are included. If the instructor suggests, accompany yourself at a piano. It will help in formulating an implied harmony—the accompaniment will strengthen a sense of implied harmony suggested by the melodic contour. Even when these melodies are not accompanied, you will begin to "imagine" implied harmony.

1 Andante con moto   Scandinavia

2 Moderato   Scandinavia

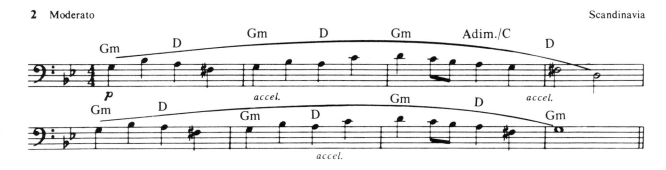

3 Adagio   Germany

4 Moderato   Norway

5 Allegretto
Russia

6 Allegro
Southern Europe

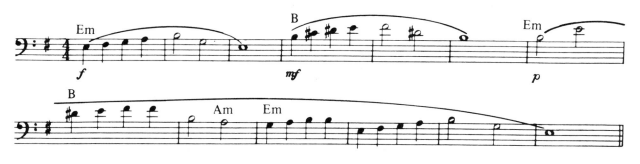

7 Moderato
United States

D. C. al Fine

8 Andante
United States

G. ET Melodic Dictation:
Using m2, M2, m3, M3, P4, P5

Each exercise consists of a short melody that begins on the tonic pitch.

1. Memorize the melody before trying to write it down.
2. If your instructor requests, sing the entire melody using solfeggio syllables or numbers. Keep trying to replace singing (out loud) with *thinking*—imagining the melody in your mind.
3. When you know the melody thoroughly, write it on the appropriate staff.

*(R) means recorded.

H. SS Melodies (Major and Minor):
P5, P4, M3, m3, M2, m2

I: Procedure for Completing Each Melody

1. These melodies are limited to the same skips as those in Unit 3, except that the skips may occur between scale tones other than 1—3—5.
2. All melodies in this section are excerpted from the songs of Franz Schubert.
3. Nearly all of the rhythms found in these melodies are presented in Section A, page 65, so you may wish to review that section before starting.
4. Numbers 6 and 9 contain a simple triplet; the three notes of the triplet should be evenly spaced over one completed beat.
5. Follow directions as printed in Unit 1, Section F, page 11.

7 Mässig   Schubert   Shepherd's Song of Lament

8 Ziemlich lebhaft   Schubert   The Son of the Muses

9 Guter Laune   Schubert   Banquet Song

II: Clef Reading

This section contains excerpts from the first movement of Schubert's Unfinished Symphony.

Procedures

1. Example 1 consists of the opening melody (mm. 13–20), played in unison by two oboes and two clarinets in A. In order to sing the clarinet part as it sounds, try to think in the soprano clef, with c′ (middle C) on the bottom line. Experiment by using letter names and by checking your accuracy with the oboe part. Remember that the oboe is a nontransposing instrument, and sounds the same pitches as the clarinet in A.

2. Example 2, from the same movement (mm. 291–98), also features different instruments playing melodies at the same pitch: violas (Vla) and cellos (Vc). Since these instruments are nontransposing, it is not necessary for you to use clefs for the purpose of changing key. Cello parts are sometimes written in the tenor clef, but most often in the bass clef.

3. In this excerpt the same melodic figure appears four times. For the purposes of this exercise, it is advised to consider the following temporary tonic pitches:

   mm. 291–92—F♯ minor
   mm. 293–94—E major
   mm. 295–96—C♯ minor
   mm. 297–98—B major

I. ET Intervals: Review (m2, M2, m3, M3, P4, P5)

Intervals studied to date: m2, M2, m3, M3, P4, P5

Each exercise consists of a single interval. The first note is given.

1. Write the second note of the interval on the staff.
2. Place the name of the interval (P4, m2, M3, etc.) in the blank provided.
3. To help you recognize intervals, think of them as parts of a scale or triad:

   P5 = tonic to 5th of a major or minor scale

   P4 = tonic to 4th scale degree of a major or minor scale

   M3 = tonic to 3rd of a major scale

   m3 = tonic to 3rd of a minor triad

   M2 = tonic to 2nd degree of a major or minor scale

   m2 = leading tone to tonic of a major or harmonic minor scale

4. In numbers 31 through 60, practice singing through the interval (think of the first pitch as tonic, and sing the successive scale degrees to the second pitch) should still be practiced. For instance, if the interval is from C down to G, sing scale degrees 8 (or 1), 7, 6, 5.
5. When you get to 5 you will notice that this pitch matches the second pitch played, and you will know that it is a P4th.
6. Remember that when singing *down,* intervals are inverted, so 5 (going up) means 4 (going down).
7. When practicing for the first time, forget about inversions and count (on your fingers) the number of scale steps you descend to match the second pitch. Later, when you have had considerable practice, experience will help you to recognize all intervals without needing to count.

21.–40. (R)

The given note is the upper note of the interval:

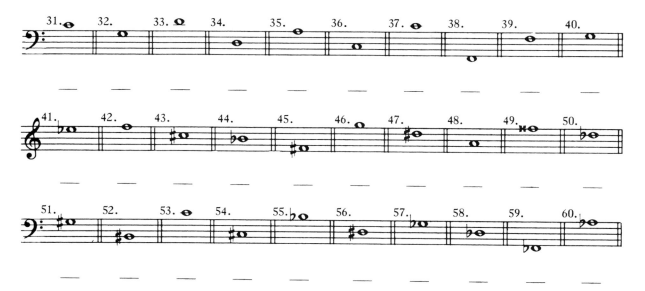

J. SS Ensemble Excerpts—Two Voices:
P5, P4, M3, m3, M2, m2

1. These melodies are similar in difficulty to those found in Section F of this unit, but you must learn to cope with another voice that will be singing different pitches.
2. Your instructor will select either two individuals or two sections of the class to sing these phrases.
3. All are excerpted from chorale melodies harmonized by Bach. Follow the directions found in Section F of this chapter.
4. Octave transposition of one of the voices may be necessary to accommodate an individual class member's range.
5. A tempo of ♩ = 72 to 80 for all examples is suggested.

4

Lord God, We Praise Thee

5

Christ, Who Art Day and Light

6

Sing the Lord a New Song

7

Mercifully Grant Us Peace

8

Christ, Who Makes Us Blessed

K. ET Chord Identification:
Major and Minor Triad Positions

Each exercise consists of the three positions of the same triad in any order. Before you begin your instructor will acquaint you with the 1–3–5–3–1 pattern, which is an essential aid in identifying the triad in root position.

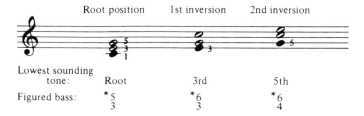

	Root position	1st inversion	2nd inversion
Lowest sounding tone:	Root	3rd	5th
Figured bass:	*$\frac{5}{3}$	*$\frac{6}{3}$	*$\frac{6}{4}$

*Indicates intervals above the lowest sounding tone

1. Listen until all three positions have been played. Locate the one in root position by relating it to the 1–3–5–3–1 pattern. Remember that 1–3–5–3–1 means that the 3rd and 5th are above the root—thus, root position.
2. When you have located the root position version write $\frac{5}{3}$ in the appropriate blank (1, 2, or 3).
3. Now that you have identified the root, 3rd, and 5th, listen a second time and sing (better yet, *think*) the 3rd of the triad. When the 3rd you are singing coincides with the lowest-sounding tone of an example, that example is in *first* inversion. Write $\frac{6}{3}$ below it.
4. Repeat the process as described in number 3, above, but this time sing the 5th of the triad. When the 5th you are singing coincides with the lowest-sounding tone of an example, that example is in *second* inversion. Write $\frac{6}{4}$ below it.
5. As you become more experienced you will discover that you can determine each position simply by listening to it as a unit—your elaborate mental calculations become automatic!

1. _____ _____ _____

2. _____ _____ _____

3. _____ _____ _____

4. _____ _____ _____

5. _____ _____ _____

6. _____ _____ _____

7. _____ _____ _____

8. _____ _____ _____

9. _____ _____ _____

10. _____ _____ _____

11.–20. (R)

11. _____ _____ _____

12. _____ _____ _____

13. _____ _____ _____

14. _____ _____ _____

15. _____ _____ _____

16. _____ _____ _____

17. _____ _____ _____

18. _____ _____ _____

19. _____ _____ _____

20. _____ _____ _____

L. ET Harmonic Function: Distinguishing among the I, ii, IV, and V Triads

Each exercise consists of a harmonic progression of four chords in four-part harmony. The harmonies are limited to the I, ii, IV, and V triads.

1. Write the roman-numeral analysis of the triads in the blanks provided.
2. Unless the instructor requests it, do not indicate inversions.
3. The example indicates the correct procedure.

EXAMPLE:

The instructor plays the following:

DM: I   ii   V   I

The student responds:

I   ii   V   I

1.–10. (R)

1. _____ _____ _____ _____   14. _____ _____ _____ _____

2. _____ _____ _____ _____   15. _____ _____ _____ _____

3. _____ _____ _____ _____   16. _____ _____ _____ _____

4. _____ _____ _____ _____   17. _____ _____ _____ _____

5. _____ _____ _____ _____   18. _____ _____ _____ _____

6. _____ _____ _____ _____   19. _____ _____ _____ _____

7. _____ _____ _____ _____   20. _____ _____ _____ _____

8. _____ _____ _____ _____   21. _____ _____ _____ _____

9. _____ _____ _____ _____   22. _____ _____ _____ _____

10. _____ _____ _____ _____   23. _____ _____ _____ _____

11. _____ _____ _____ _____   24. _____ _____ _____ _____

12. _____ _____ _____ _____   25. _____ _____ _____ _____

13. _____ _____ _____ _____

5

A. SS Rhythm: Introduction of the Triplet

I

Consider each measure as a module to be sung separately or as part of a series.

1. Follow procedures given in Unit 2, Section A, page 23.
2. If your instructor recommends, conduct yourself using the hand movements illustrated in Unit 1, page 2.

Rhythm syllables:

1 an du 2 an du 3 an du
1 la le 2 la le 3 la le

Pronunciation:

AN as in *ANOTHER*
DU as in *DUMP*
LA as in *LARVA*
LE as in *LEE*

Some illustrations:

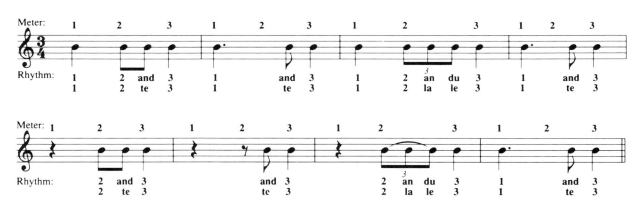

II

Sing the following exercises on a neutral pitch:

1. Clap the meter.
   Say the rhythm using rhythm syllables.
2. Say the meter using numbers.
   Clap the rhythm.
3. Tap the meter with one hand.
   Tap the rhythm with the other hand.
4. Half the class taps the meter.

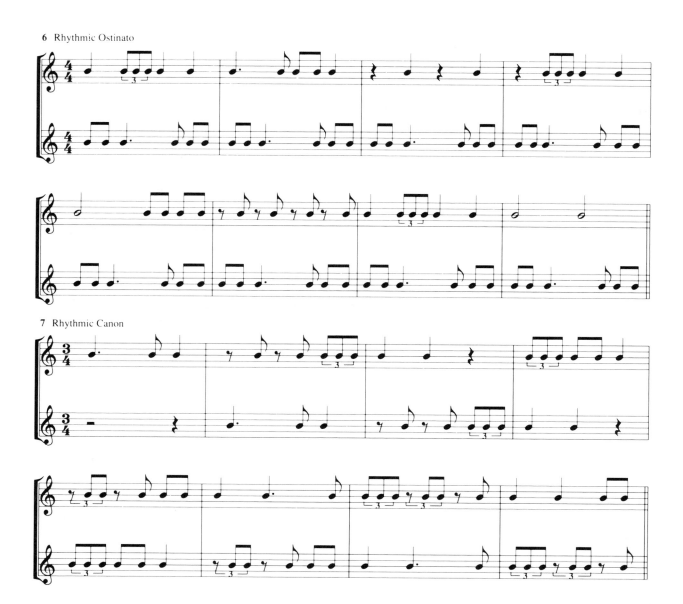

B. ET Rhythmic Dictation: Introduction
of Quarter-Beat Values

Each exercise is a short melodic phrase. Numbers 1–12 consist of two measures each and are intended to introduce quarter-beat values. Numbers 13–22 are taken from music literature.

1. Complete each rhythm on the single line provided.
2. The value of the first note is given in all exercises.

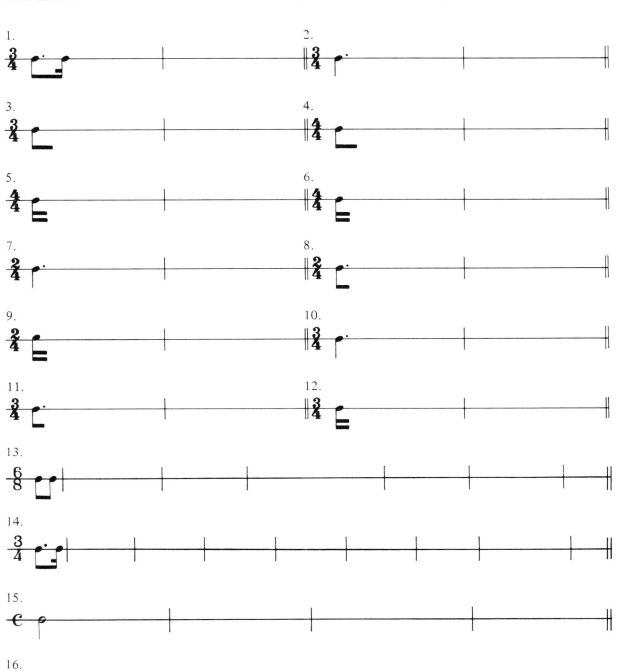

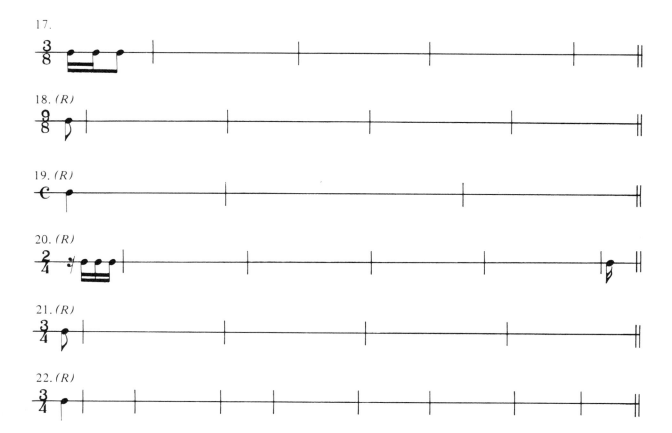

C. SS Diatonic Models for Interval Study
New Intervals: M6, m6
Review: m10, P8, P5, P4, M3, m3, M2, m2

I

Emphasis on intervals of the major 6th (M6) and minor 6th (m6).

Exercises 1–5

The exercises in this section relate to the music of Chopin, with particular emphasis on the interval of the M6th. These exercises correspond with the melodic fragments quoted in Section D (page 96) of this unit.

Exercises 1–3 emphasize the 3rd scale degree. In exercise 3, the motion moves from scale degree 3 (A) to 1 (F) by means of a passing-tone figure. The ability to hear the structural significance of scale degree 3 in this context will assist you in singing melody no. 1 in Section D of this unit.

Follow the same procedure as in previous units. For extra practice, sing exercises 4 and 5 in all major keys, transposing to each new key by P5ths down or P4ths up. If you feel reckless, and your instructor does not get caught with cosmic debris, try tossing triads (exercises 4 and 5) at each other using the following illustration. It shows you how to get from F major to E♭ major (through B♭). You should be able to go nine keys beyond those keys in the following model:

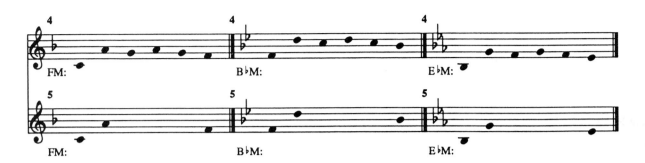

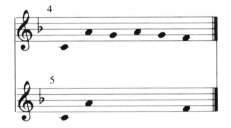

Exercises 6–12

These emphasize the M6th as the opening interval. The stemmed notes of exercises 6–10 outline a tonic triad. You will find this melodic fragment as no. 2 in Section D (page 96) of this unit. All of the procedures used with previous exercises apply here as well, including the extra practice patterns of exercises 11–12.

Exercises:

Exercises 13–16

Here the minor 6th (m6) is a chordal skip. The minor 6th in exercise 14 (F down to A) functions as a consonant skip in support of the final pitch, C. Exercises 15 and 16 provide opportunities for repeating patterns at the 5th. Likewise, the triad in exercise 16 could also be tossed around in a similar manner—watch out for window glass. This melodic fragment appears in Section D as Melody no. 3. The following is an illustration of the transposition pattern you should follow (but go beyond):

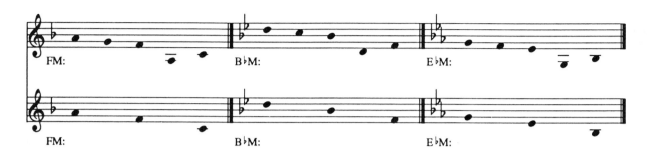

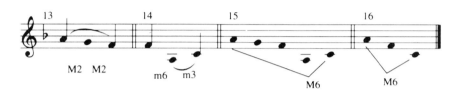

Exercises 17–24

In this set, the major 6th (M6) is part of III in pure (natural) minor. Exercises 17–24 imply III (major triad) in D minor. This melodic pattern appears in Section D as Melody no. 4. Use the same procedures as found earlier. The following model shows you how to move from D minor to F minor—through G and C minor. You can go to eight additional keys:

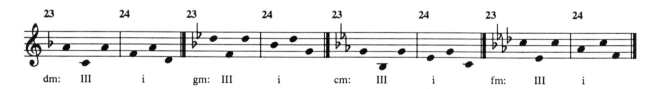

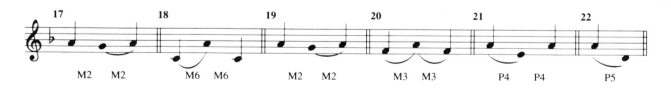

Exercises 25–29

The sequential relationship of exercises 25–27 (F major) with triads on F and D is similar to that of the previous example, except that the tonic of the previous exercise is D minor. Use the same procedures as earlier. For extra practice, take exercises 25 and 27 and repeat the combined patterns down a P5th or up a P4th. The following model shows how to start the procedure:

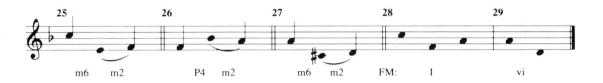

Exercises 30–36

These exercises outline the D-minor tonic triad. Use exercise 36 as the basis for singing the pattern in each key. Please see the following model.

In this unit, the authors recommend drills in relative minor rather than parallel minor, because of the tonal design of melodic fragments 4 and 5, which begin in F major and end in D minor.

II: Alto Clef*

As advised in Unit 1, Section C, you should now return to the familiar diatonic models of Unit 1, Section C for practice in clef reading.

In numbers 1–26, just to show your versatility, substitute the alto clef for the treble clef and change the key signature—see the model:

CM: = DM: CM: = DM:

D. SS Melodic Fragments for Interval Singing
New Intervals: M6, m6
Review: m10, P8, P5, P4, M3, m3, M2, m2

Sing the following excerpts using correct rhythm and pitch.

(Note to the instructor: Relate the following melodies to the exercises in Section C, page 92.)

1   Andante ♪ = 132   Chopin Nocturne, op. 9, no. 2 (transposed)

2   Lento   Chopin Nocturne, op. 62, no. 2 (transposed)

3   Lento sostenuto ♩. = 50   Chopin Nocturne, op. 27, no. 2 (transposed)

4   Lento ♩. = 60   Chopin Nocturne, op. 15, no. 3 (transposed)

5   Lento sostenuto   Chopin Nocturne, op. 55, no. 2 (transposed)

6   Allegro molto agitato ♩. = 96   Chopin Etude, op. 10, no. 9 (transposed)

E. ET Models and Embellishments:
Descending 6ths in Two Voices

1. Notice that the model in this section is made up of two voices that descend in parallel 6ths. Sing both parts of this structure before class.
2. Your instructor will play the structure followed by embellishments of that structure.
3. Write the model's embellishments on the numbered staves provided.

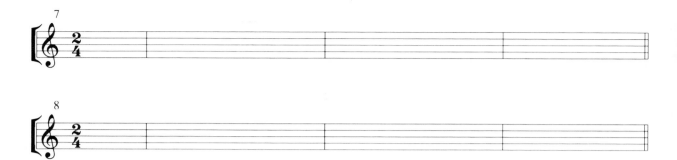

F. SS Melodies (Folk Songs): P5, P4, M3, m3, M2, m2

Procedure for Completing Each Melody

1. These melodies are limited to the same skips as those in Unit 4. All are folk songs.
2. All of the rhythms found in these melodies were presented in previous units.
3. Follow directions as printed in Unit 4, Section F, page 72.

9 ♩ – 132   Folk Song   United States

10   Folk Song   United States

G. ET Melodic Dictation: Scalewise Passages and Arpeggiations of I and V

Each exercise consists of a short melodic phrase. Complete the phrase on the staff in notation.

1. As you listen to each melody the first time, try to memorize it immediately in its entirety.
2. Do *not* try to write anything on paper yet! You will learn almost nothing by trying to write too early.
3. Before you hear the melody a second time, sing as much of it (from first hearing) as you can.
4. A second or third hearing should provide the pitches you missed, so you are probably able to sing the entire melody from memory now.
5. Listen as many times as you need to in order to memorize the entire melody.
6. Only after you have the entire melody memorized should you attempt to write anything on paper!
7. Observe that when you have the melody memorized, you can slow it down sufficiently to write the notes on the staff as you sing (or preferably *think*).
8. Write the melody on the staff in music notation.

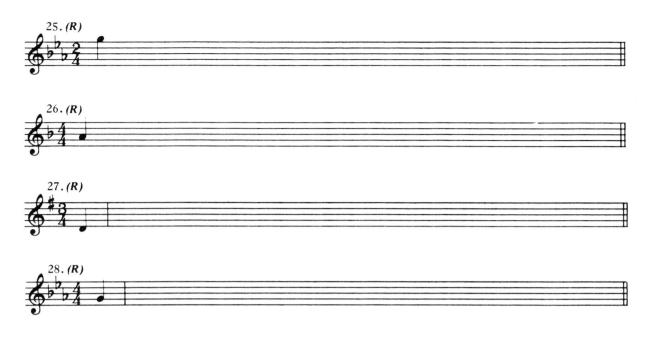

*(R) means recorded.

H. SS Melodies: P5, P4, M3, m3, M2, m2

I

1. Because of an occasional M6 or m6 skip, it is suggested that Section C of this unit be practiced before singing these melodies.
2. All of the rhythms found in these melodies are presented in Unit 4, Section A, page 65.
3. Follow directions as given in Unit 4, Section F, page 72.
4. Chord symbols above the staves are found in selected melodies in this as well as ensuing units. The purpose of these symbols is to increase awareness of implied harmony created by the melody notes. The ability to imagine (tonal imagery) or "think" the accompanying harmony helps one to understand and sing a melody more accurately. These symbols may be utilized in any of the following ways:
   a. Some class members sing the melody while others sing only the symbols (as root-position harmony).
   b. One member of the class (using the chord symbols) accompanies the melodies at a piano.
   c. The instructor may elect to accompany the melodies at the piano.
   d. Individual class members sing duets—one singing the melody while the other sings the tones represented by the chord symbols.

1 Andante   France

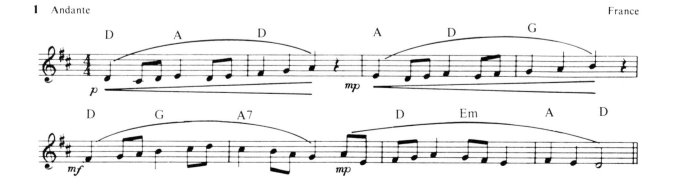

5 Allegretto

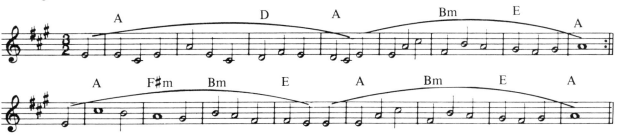

6 ♩. - 66

Dowland *Now, O Now I Needs Must Part*

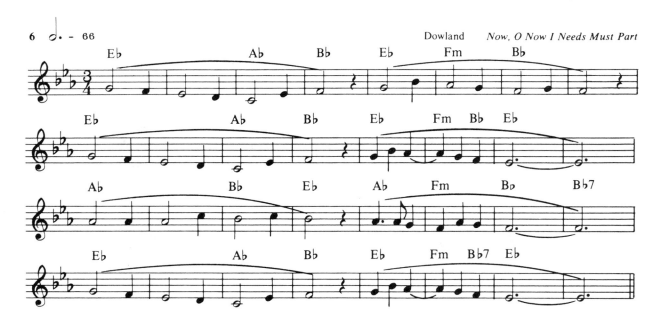

7 Moderato

8 ♩ – 126   Rosa   *To Be Near the Fair Idol*

9 𝅗𝅥 – 69   Savile   *Here's Health Unto His Majesty*

10 ♪ – 144   Beethoven   *Mutual Love*

11 ♩ - 138   Beethoven   *German Dance*

12 ♩ - 120   von Weber

13 ♩ - 138   Dandrieu

II: Clef Reading

Two selections from Schumann's *Album for the Young,* op. 68 provide further exercises in clef reading.

Example 1: This excerpt is in A B A form. The melody of the B section is the same as A except that it centers around G as tonic rather than C. With the return of the original material in the final A, the bass clef is used to illustrate the 5th relationship between the bass and tenor clefs.

Example 2: This illustrates "clef mania." Line 2 is almost identical to line 1 (except for its octave transposition), and allows you to check to see if you are reading the clef correctly. The only new clef is the mezzo-soprano clef, which places middle C (c′) on the second line up from the lowest.

1 Nicht schnell — Schumann op. 68, no. 3 Humming Tune

P 5th

(Sing this line an octave higher)

2 Frisch und fröhlich — Schumann op. 68, no. 8 "The Mad Horseman"

(Sing this line an octave higher)

I. ET Scale Degrees: Two-Note Groups

1. The instructor first plays a scale, then two tones of that scale.
2. Identify the two scale degrees played. The instructor will tell you whether to use scale numbers or syllables.
3. Review Unit 2, Section I.

The instructor plays this scale.

1. _____	6. _____	11. _____	16. _____
2. _____	7. _____	12. _____	17. _____
3. _____	8. _____	13. _____	18. _____
4. _____	9. _____	14. _____	19. _____
5. _____	10. _____	15. _____	20. _____

J. SS Ensemble Excerpts—Two Voices:
P5, P4, M3, m3

Procedure

1. These melodies are similar in difficulty to those found in Section F of this chapter, but you must now learn to cope with another voice that will be singing different pitches.
2. Follow procedures outlined in Unit 4, Section J, page 82.
3. Octave transposition of one of the voices may be necessary to accommodate individual class member's range.

1   Beethoven

2   Wachsmann

3   Folk Song

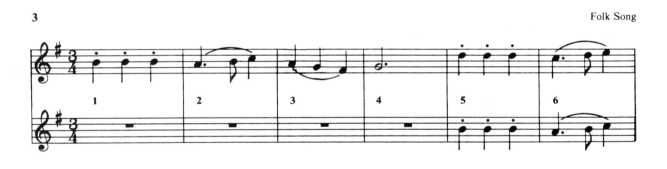

Folk Song

Clementi Sonatina, op. 36, no. 6 (adapted)

Canonic Imitation

Canonic Imitation

Bach   *Lord Christ, the Only Son of God*

Bach   *Be Glad, My Soul*

K. ET Chord Identification: Triad Positions

Each exercise is a single triad in four-part harmony. Indicate the triad position. Your answers should be:

root position $= \frac{5}{3}$

first inversion $= \frac{6}{3}$

second inversion $= \frac{6}{4}$

The techniques in Unit 4, Section K will help you.

Example:

1. _____   11. _____

2. _____   12. _____

3. _____   13. _____

4. _____   14. _____

5. _____   15. _____

6. _____   16. _____

7. _____   17. _____

8. _____   18. _____

9. _____   19. _____

10. _____   20. _____

L. ET Harmonic Function: I(i), ii(ii°), IV(iv), and V Triads and Inversions

Each exercise consists of a series of four chords in block harmony.

In the blanks provided, write the analysis of each of the four chords.

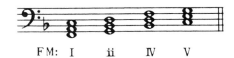

F M: I   ii   IV   V

1.–10. (R)

1. _____ _____ _____ _____   9. _____ _____ _____ _____

2. _____ _____ _____ _____   10. _____ _____ _____ _____

3. _____ _____ _____ _____   11. _____ _____ _____ _____

4. _____ _____ _____ _____   12. _____ _____ _____ _____

5. _____ _____ _____ _____   13. _____ _____ _____ _____

6. _____ _____ _____ _____   14. _____ _____ _____ _____

7. _____ _____ _____ _____   15. _____ _____ _____ _____

8. _____ _____ _____ _____

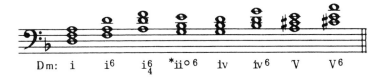

D m: i   i⁶   i⁶₄   *ii°⁶   iv   iv⁶   V   V⁶

16. _____ _____ _____ _____   21. _____ _____ _____ _____

17. _____ _____ _____ _____   22. _____ _____ _____ _____

18. _____ _____ _____ _____   23. _____ _____ _____ _____

19. _____ _____ _____ _____   24. _____ _____ _____ _____

20. _____ _____ _____ _____   25. _____ _____ _____ _____

6

A. SS Rhythm: More Difficult Quarter-Beat Values

I

Consider each measure as a module to be sung separately or as part of a series.

Follow procedures given in Unit 2, Section A, page 23. Work continually for both accuracy and speed—with accuracy taking precedence.

For rhythm syllables, see Unit 4, Section A, page 65.

II

See directions in Unit 5, Section A, part II, page 88.

2   Rhythmic Crescendo and Decrescendo

6 The upper voice is a rhythmic augmentation of the first four bars of the lower voice

7 Rhythmic Ostinato

B. ET Rhythmic Dictation: Quarter-Beat Values

Each exercise consists of a two-measure melody.

Complete the rhythm on a neutral pitch.

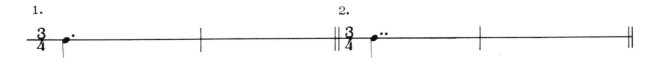

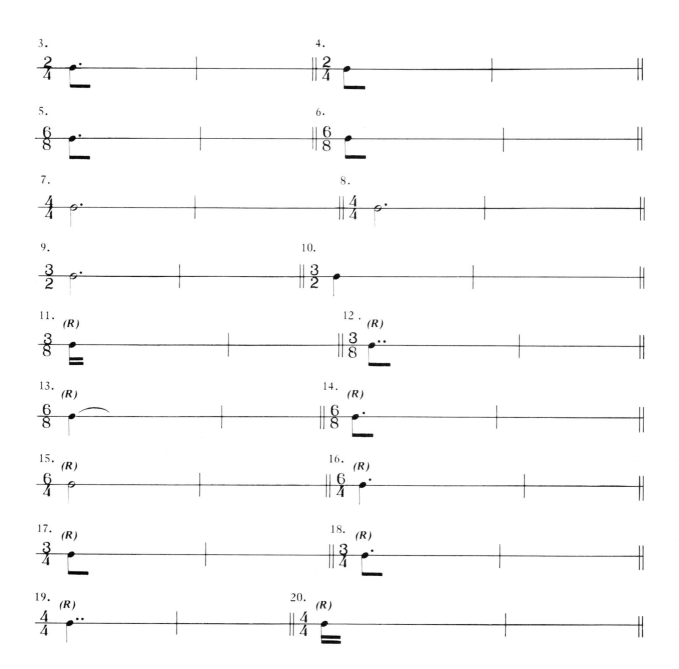

C. SS Diatonic Models for Interval Study
Review: M6, m6

I

Review of intervals of the major and minor 6th. The exercises in this section relate to a large number of composers, including Mozart, Beethoven, Mussorgsky, and others. These exercises correspond with the melodic fragments quoted in Section D (page 121) of this unit.

Exercises 1–5

Exercises 1–5 emphasize the chordal skips within a major tonic triad starting with the root, moving down to the fifth, and then up to the third. The upward skip from scale degree 5 to scale degree 3 results in the interval of a major 6th (M6).

Follow the same procedures as in previous chapters. For extra practice sing exercise 5 in all major keys, transposing to each new key by P5ths down or P4ths up. The tossing of triads among students ought to continue as illustrated in the following model:

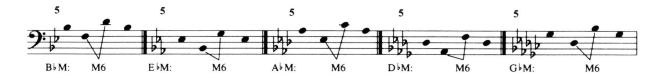

The first three melodic fragments (Mozart, Beethoven, and Makeba) of Section D follow a similar melodic contour. Therefore, exercises 1–5 (of this section) will apply to fragments 1–3 (of Section D).

Exercises 6–15

Exercises 6–15 emphasize the choral skips within a major tonic triad starting with the root, moving to the third, and then down to the fifth. The downward skip from scale degree 3 to scale degree 5 results in a major 6th. In comparing exercises 2 and 7, note the reordering of pitches (F, D, F in exercise 2) and (D, F, D in exercise 7).

Follow the same procedures as in previous units. Sing no. 15 in all major keys, transposing in the manner described in each previous unit. The tonic and subdominant triads are outlined. The dominant is implied only with the leading tone as it progresses to tonic. Please see the following model:

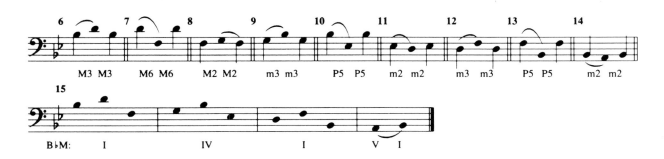

Exercises 16–23

These exercises combine the major and minor 6th patterns that form the basis of melodic fragments 5, 6, and 7 of Section D (page 121).

Follow the same procedure as described in previous units, using exercise 23 as the model for transposition. The tossing of major and minor triads may provide even more cosmic debris than in previous exercises.

Illustration of transpositional pattern:

Melodic fragments 5, 6, and 7 (Section D) focus on the ascending minor 6th within the G-minor tonic triad.

Exercises (apply to fragments 5, 6, and 7 of Section D):

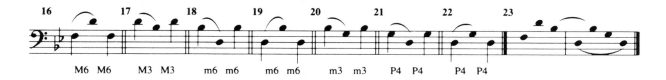

Exercise 24

This emphasizes the ascending major 6th (M6) followed by a descending scale line, and may be thought of in Bb major as well as G minor. Exercise 24 is related to fragments 8–10 of Section D (page 122). Concentrate on the Bb that may be scale degree 3 (in G minor) and 1 in (Bb major).

II Alto Clef*

Now return to the familiar diatonic models of Unit 2, Section C (page 32) for practice in clef reading. In numbers 1–39, substitute the alto clef for the treble clef and change the key signature. See the following model:

D. SS Melodic Fragments for Interval Singing
Review: M6, m6

Sing the following excerpts using correct rhythm and pitch.

(Note to the instructor: Relate the following melodies to exercises in Section C, page 118.)

Exercises:

8 Andante (♩ = 80)   Tchaikovsky   Symphony no. 5, op. 64 (transposed)

9 Allegro   Mozart   Six German Dances, no. V, KV 509 (transposed)

10 With easy gaiety   Mahler   "Up There on the Hill" (transposed)

E. ET Models and Embellishments:
5–6 Patterns in Two Voices

1. Notice that the model in this section is made up of two voices that ascend in oblique motion. Sing both parts of this structure before class.
2. Your instructor will play the structure followed by embellishments of that structure.
3. Write the model's embellishments on the numbered staves provided.

5   A five-measure example based on the same model.

F. SS Melodies for Review and Practice in Singing at Performance Tempo

Procedure for Completing Each Melody

1. These melodies are easy enough to be sung at performance tempo without rehearsal. See if you can sing each without error on the first try.
2. All rhythms and intervals have been studied in prior units.

1   Allegro   United States

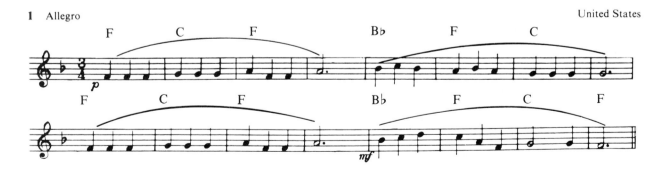

2 Moderato

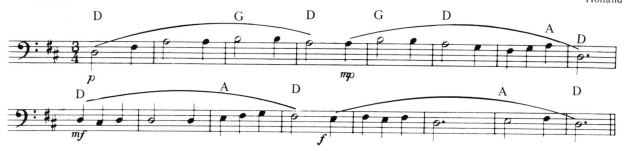

Holland

3 Allegro

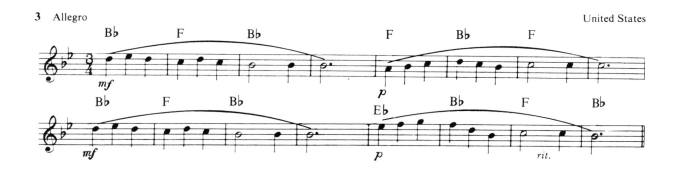

United States

4 Moderato

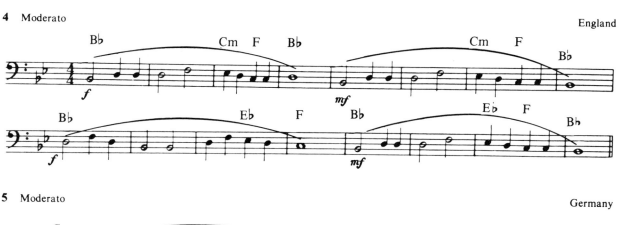

England

5 Moderato

Germany

6 Moderato Alaska

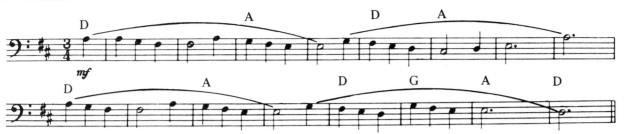

7 Andante Canada

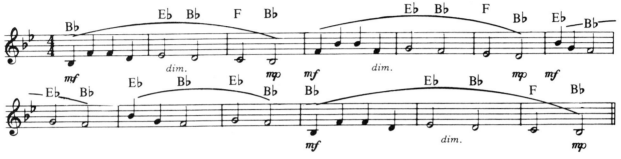

8 Allegretto South Europe

9 Lively France

10 Allegro

France

11 ♩ - 138

J.C. Bach *Peasant Dance*

12 ♩ - 144

De Lubin *Old Polish Dance*

13 ♩ - 112

Bach *Awaken, My Heart*

14 ♩ - 144

Muller *Serenade*

G. ET Melodic Dictation: Melodies Outlining the I, IV, V (and vii°6) Triads

Each exercise consists of a short melody.

Complete the composition on the staff in notation.

*(R) means recorded.

H. SS Melodies for Careful Study and Preparation

Procedure for Completing Each Melody

1. These melodies are somewhat more difficult than those in Section F of this unit, and should be carefully prepared.
2. All rhythms and intervals have been studied in prior units.
3. Follow directions found in Unit 3, Section F, page 54. If needed, circle reference tones (scale degrees 1,3, and 5) in preparation for singing.

1 Moderato
England

2 ♩ – 120
Purcell *Mad Bess*

3 ♩ – 84
Horn *Cherry Ripe*

4 ♩ – 84
Haydn Symphony no. 101 in D Major

5 ♩ – 126-144
Schumann *Papillons*

6 Moderato England

7 ♩ - 63-88   Clementi   *Trumpet Call Sonata*

8 ♩ - 66   Schumann   *A Little Piece*

9 Andante

Transpose this familiar Rossini tune up a minor second to F major, starting on note C, by reading in the alto clef (displaced by an octave).

10 Allegro vivace
Rossini William Tell Overture, R-10

* Ten measures omitted

11 Schubert *Ecossaise* I, D. 421

(meas. 1-4) * octave lower than original

12 Bach English Suite III, *Gavotte II* (or Musette)

*(eight measures omitted)

13 Brandenburg Concerto no. 2, I (transposed down two octaves)

in waltz time ♩= 112
meas. 7

Samuel Barber   "Under the Willow Tree" from *Vanessa*

"Under The Willow Tree" From *Vanessa*. Music by Samuel Barber. Copyright © 1939 (Renewed) G. Schirmer, Inc. International Copyright Secured. All Rights Reserved. Used by permission.

I. ET New Intervals: m6 and M6

Each exercise consists of a single interval. The first note is given.

1.   Write the second note of the interval on the staff.
2.   Place the name of the interval (P4, m6, M6, etc.) in the blank provided.
3.   To help you recognize the new intervals, think of them as parts of a scale:

Second note ABOVE the first: M6 = tonic to 6th of a major scale

Second note BELOW the first: M6 = when you hear the second pitch, think of it as the tonic of a major scale

Second note above the first: m6 = tonic to 6th of a minor scale

Second note below the first: m6 = when you hear the second pitch, think of it as the tonic of a minor scale

The given note is the lower of the two.

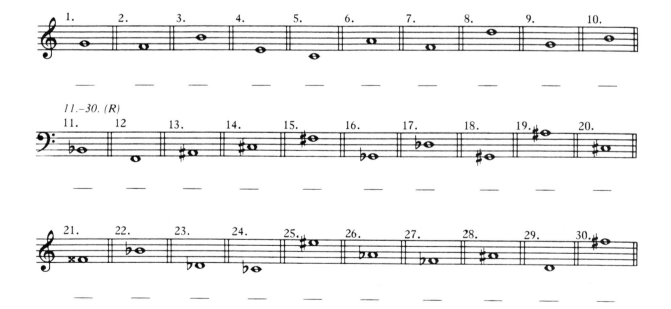

The given note is the upper of the two.

J. SS Ensemble Excerpts for Review—
Two Voices with One Excerpt in Four Voices

Procedure

1. These melodies are similar in difficulty to those found in Section F.
2. Follow procedures outlined in Unit 4, Section J, page 82.
3. Octave transposition of one of the voices may be necessary to accommodate individual class member's ranges.

1   Andante (♩ = 86)   Béla Bartók *Mikrokosmos, Vol. II (Méditation)*

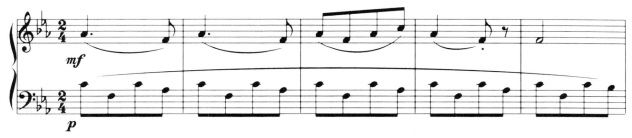

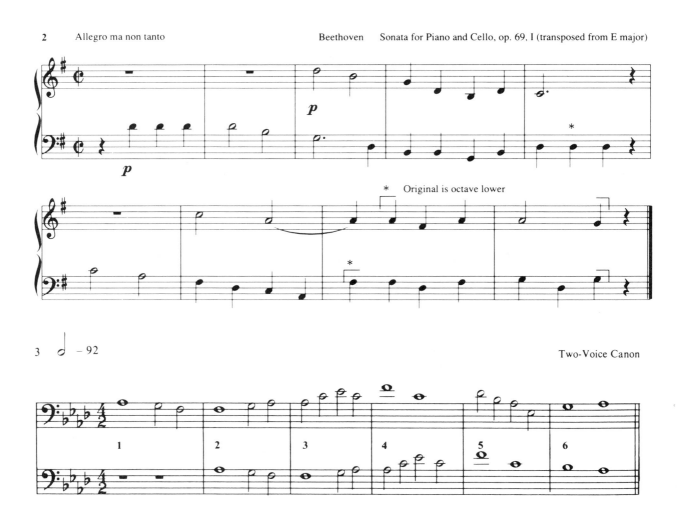

2   Allegro ma non tanto   Beethoven   Sonata for Piano and Cello, op. 69, I (transposed from E major)

*   Original is octave lower

3   ♩ – 92   Two-Voice Canon

4

Folk Song   *The Two Sisters* (pentatonic scale)

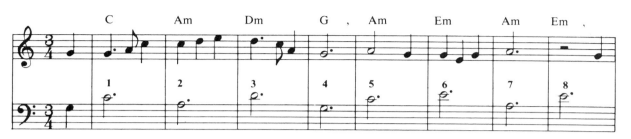

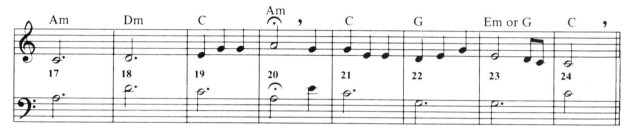

5

Bach

Folk Song   *Blow the Candles Out* (Dorian mode)

7

D. Scarlatti

8

Mozart   String Quartet, K. 458, I (transposed)

K. ET Triad Factor Identification: Factors in the Soprano and Bass Voices

Each exercise consists of a single triad played in four-part harmony.

1. Indicate the chord factor (1–3–5) in the soprano voice.
2. Indicate the chord factor (1–3–5) in the bass voice.

11.–20. (R)

1. _____   6. _____   11. _____   16. _____

2. _____   7. _____   12. _____   17. _____

3. _____   8. _____   13. _____   18. _____

4. _____   9. _____   14. _____   19. _____

5. _____   10. _____   15. _____   20. _____

L. ET Harmonic Function: I, ii, IV, V, and vi Triads

Each exercise consists of four block chords in four-part harmony.

Write the roman-numeral analysis of each chord in the blanks provided.

Numbers 1–15 contain root-position triads only:

1.–10. (R)

1. ____ ____ ____ ____   9. ____ ____ ____ ____

2. ____ ____ ____ ____   10. ____ ____ ____ ____

3. ____ ____ ____ ____   11. ____ ____ ____ ____

4. ____ ____ ____ ____   12. ____ ____ ____ ____

5. ____ ____ ____ ____   13. ____ ____ ____ ____

6. ____ ____ ____ ____   14. ____ ____ ____ ____

7. ____ ____ ____ ____   15. ____ ____ ____ ____

8. ____ ____ ____ ____

Numbers 16–25 contain inversions:

16. ____ ____ ____ ____   21. ____ ____ ____ ____

17. ____ ____ ____ ____   22. ____ ____ ____ ____

18. ____ ____ ____ ____   23. ____ ____ ____ ____

19. ____ ____ ____ ____   24. ____ ____ ____ ____

20. ____ ____ ____ ____   25. ____ ____ ____ ____

7

A. SS Rhythm: Review of Previous Rhythms with Emphasis on the Triplet

I

1. Consider each measure as a module to be practiced separately or as part of a series requested by your instructor.
2. Follow procedures outlined in Unit 2, Section A, page 23. Work continually for both accuracy and speed—with accuracy taking precedence.

II

Directions: Same as for Unit 5, Section A, page 87.

4

5

6 Rhythmic Canon

B. ET Rhythmic Dictation: Beat Units Divided into Triplets

Each exercise consists of a short phrase of music.

Indicate the rhythm on the staff using a neutral pitch. The value for the first note(s) is given.

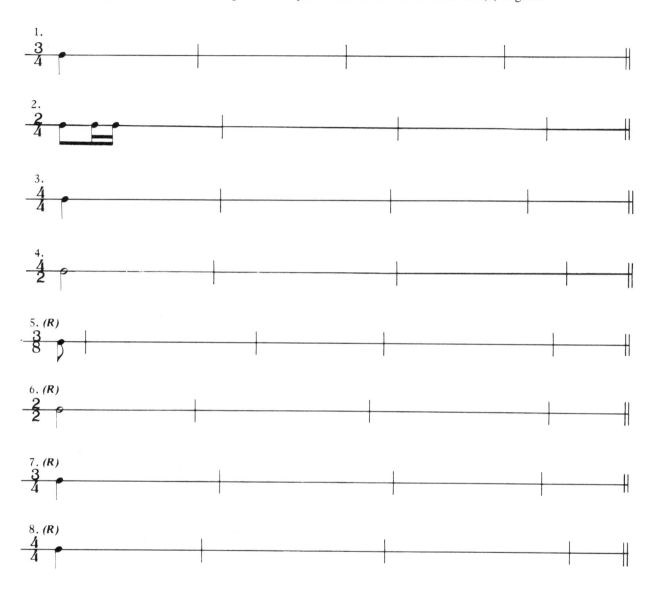

C. SS Diatonic Models for Interval Study
New Interval: m7
Review: P8

I

Emphasis on the interval of a minor 7th (m7).

The exercises in this section relate to the music of Haydn, Mozart, and Beethoven, with particular emphasis on the m7th. The musical fragments that correspond with these exercises are quoted in Section D (page 145) of this unit.

Exercises 1–6

Exercises 1–5 stress the P5th and m7th and outline the contour of melodic fragment 1 (page 145).
Exercise 6 represents an expansion of exercise 5 and outlines the opening theme of Mozart's "A Little Night Music," fragment 2 (page 145) of this unit, and also fragment 1 of Unit 4, Section D.

Follow the same procedures as in previous units. For extra practice in antiphonal singing, try the following: (1) sing exercise 5, (2) another class member sings exercise 6 in the same key, (3) then sing this antiphonal exercise in all major keys, transposing to each new key by P5ths down or P4ths up. Please use the following model:

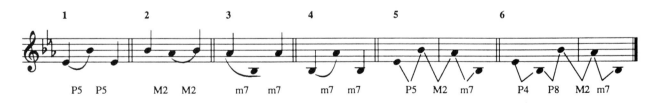

Exercises 7–12

Exercises 7–11 outline fragment 3 from Mozart's Horn Concerto, K. 447 (page 145), with special emphasis on the ascending scale passage that outlines a major 6th. Exercise 12 represents a reordering of exercise 11 in that the major 6th is inverted to become a minor 3rd. Exercise 12 outlines fragment 4 (page 146) also from Mozart's K. 447.

Use exercises 11 and 12 as another exercise in antiphonal singing (directions, page 143). Please see the following model:

Exercises 13–18

These exercises reverse the harmonic process of the previous exercises. Rather than moving from tonic to dominant, these move from dominant to tonic. Minor 7ths are emphasized. Exercises 13–17 follow the contour of fragment 5 (page 146), while exercise 18 is in preparation for fragment 6 (page 146).

Previous procedures apply here, including antiphonal singing. Please see the following model:

Exercises 19–24

These exercises follow the contour of fragments 7 and 8 (page 146). Follow previous procedures except for antiphonal singing since exercise 24 represents both excerpts. Please see the following model:

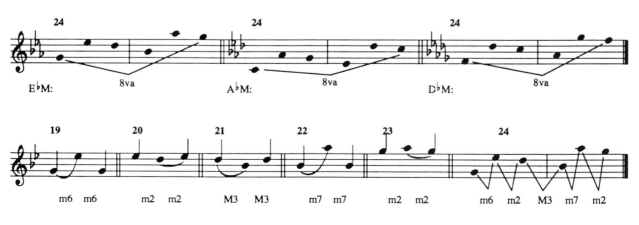

The last three melodic fragments (9, 10, and 11) in Section D are further illustrations of patterns already presented.

II Alto Clef*

Return now to the familiar diatonic models of Unit 3, Section C (page 52) for practice in clef reading. In numbers 1–35, just to show your versatility, substitute the alto clef for the given clef and change the key signature (see the following model):

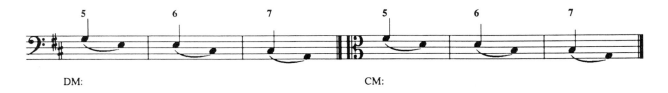

D. SS Melodic Fragments for Interval Singing
New Interval: m7

Sing the following excerpts using correct rhythm and pitch.

(Note to the instructor: Relate the following melodies to exercises in Section C, page 143.)

1   Andante   Haydn   Symphony no. 94 (second movement – transposed)

2   Allegro   Mozart   "A Little Night Music," K.525 (transposed)

3   Allegro   Mozart   Horn Concerto, K.447 (first movement)

E. ET Models and Embellishments:
7–3 Patterns in Two Voices

1. Notice that the model in this section is made up of two voices that move in similar and oblique motion, forming 7ths and 3rds. Sing both parts of this structure before class.
2. Your instructor will play the structure followed by embellishments of that structure.
3. Write the model's embellishments on the numbered staves provided.

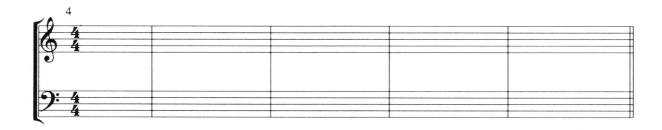

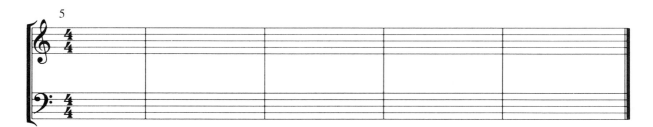

F. SS Melodies for Review and Practice in Singing at Performance Tempo

1. These melodies are easy enough to be sung at performance tempo without rehearsal.
2. Nevertheless, a ten-second scrutiny to determine difficult skips or an unusual rhythm is a reasonable strategy.
3. All rhythms and intervals have been studied in prior units.
4. Numbers 11–24 are shorter than those that precede them and afford an opportunity for practicing increased tempi.

3 Sostenuto   Beethoven   Three Sonatas, no. 3, II, Var. II, WoO47

4   Beethoven   Three Sonatas, no. 3, Var. VI, WoO47

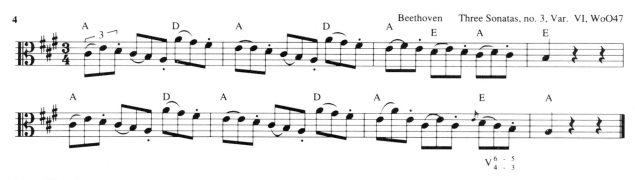

5 Plaintive

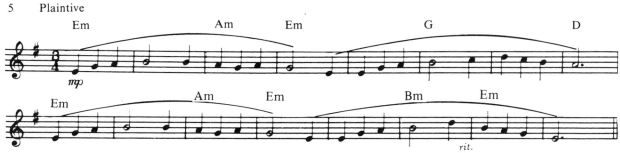

6 Andante

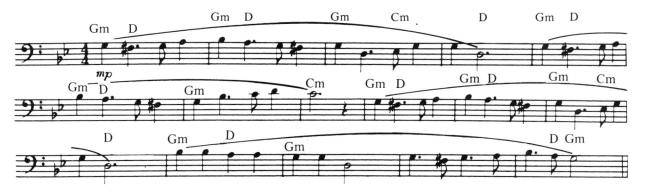

7 Andante con Moto

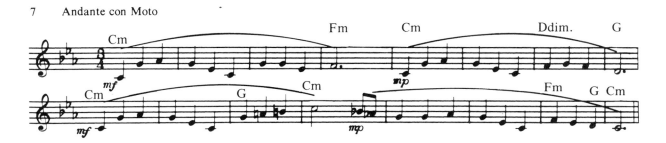

G. ET Melodic Dictation: Intervals of a 7th

Each exercise consists of a short melody. Numbers 1–10 introduce the intervals of a 7th, while numbers 11–18 are excerpted from the works of J. S. Bach.

1. After hearing each melody, try immediately to sing it in its entirety in your mind (aural imagery).
2. When that is accomplished, add solfeggio syllables or numbers as you think the melody through again.
3. Do not write out the melody until you have completed these two important procedures.
4. Complete each melody on the staff in notation. The first note(s) is given for each. Incomplete final measures are marked "inc."

In numbers 1–10 the given pitch is the tone:

*(R) means recorded.

H. SS Melodies for Careful Study and Preparation

Procedure for Completing Each Melody

1. These melodies are selected from instrumental literature. They are somewhat more difficult than those in Section F of this unit, and will require more careful attention.
2. All rhythms and intervals have been studied in prior units.
3. Follow directions found in Unit 2, Section F, page 34. If necessary, circle reference tones (scale degrees 1, 3, and 5) in preparation for singing.

1   Handel   Suite in D minor, Variation 4

2   Handel   Suite in D minor, Sarabande

3   Handel   Minuet in G minor

4   Handel   Chaconne in G major

5   Handel   Suite, Menuetto

6   Handel   Suite in G major, Gigue

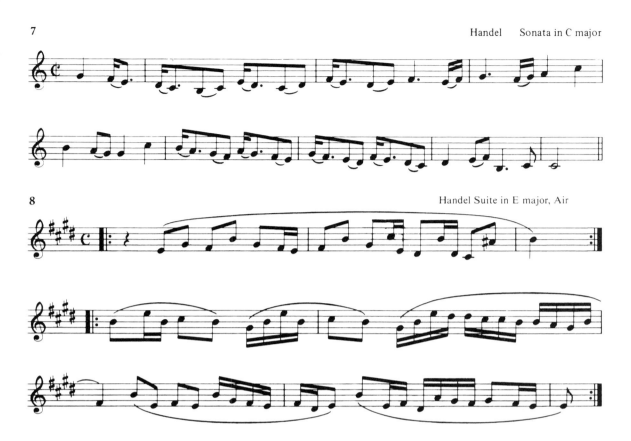

7   Handel   Sonata in C major

8   Handel Suite in E major, Air

I. ET Scale Degrees: Three-Note Groups

1. The instructor first plays a scale, then three tones of that scale.
2. Identify the three scale degrees played. The instructor will tell you whether to use scale numbers or syllables.

The instructor plays this scale:

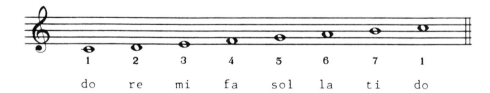

These tones are in ascending order:

1. _____ _____ _____
2. _____ _____ _____
3. _____ _____ _____
4. _____ _____ _____
5. _____ _____ _____
6. _____ _____ _____
7. _____ _____ _____
8. _____ _____ _____
9. _____ _____ _____
10. _____ _____ _____
11. _____ _____ _____
12. _____ _____ _____
13. _____ _____ _____
14. _____ _____ _____
15. _____ _____ _____
16. _____ _____ _____

These tones are in mixed ascending and descending order:

17. _____ _____ _____
18. _____ _____ _____
19. _____ _____ _____
20. _____ _____ _____
21. _____ _____ _____
22. _____ _____ _____
23. _____ _____ _____
24. _____ _____ _____
25. _____ _____ _____
26. _____ _____ _____
27. _____ _____ _____
28. _____ _____ _____
29. _____ _____ _____
30. _____ _____ _____
31. _____ _____ _____
32. _____ _____ _____

J. SS Ensemble Excerpts—Two and Three Voices

Procedure

1. These melodies are similar in difficulty to those found in Section F.
2. Follow procedures outlined in Unit 4, Section J, page 82.
3. Some of the excerpts will permit octave transposition of one of the voices to accommodate individual class member's range.

1   Couperin

A. Scarlatti

Composition number 3 in this section is a *round*. The first voice begins, and when it reaches "2" the second voice begins at "1." When the first voice reaches "3" the third voice begins at "1." The composition ends when the first voice sings "3" (last phrase) for the second time.

Numbers refer to the marked sections of the music:

First voice:	1 2 3 1 2 3 end
Second voice:	1 2 3 1 2 end
Third voice:	1 2 3 1 end

3   Cherubini

This is an interesting excerpt because, according to the directions, it may be sung forward and backward, then turned upside down and sung both forward and backward. The text translates freely: "You should dedicate yourself entirely to your art."

4

Haydn

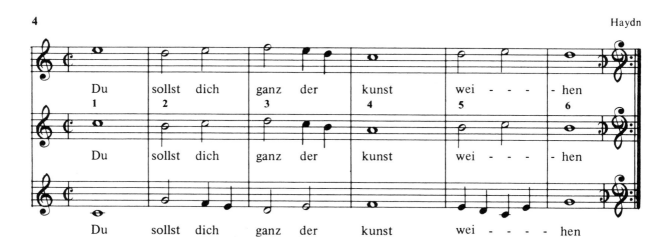

Du sollst dich ganz der kunst wei - - - - hen

Du sollst dich ganz der kunst wei - - - - hen

Du sollst dich ganz der kunst wei - - - - hen

5 𝅗𝅥 - 80

Canon at the Octave

Transpose this familiar melody down a major second to G by reading the upper line in tenor clef (*for these purposes,* the 4th line is c'', an 8ve higher, than c') and the lower line in alto clef (*for these purposes,* the middle line is c, an 8ve lower than c').

6

Bach   A canon from *In dulci jubilo*   (double canon at 8ve), Vol. II

Inner voices omitted

K. ET Nonharmonic Tones: Introduction

Each exercise consists of a nonharmonic tone in a two-voice setting. Write the name of the nonharmonic tone in the appropriate blank.

1. Nonharmonic tones played in this section are:
   Unaccented passing tone
   Unaccented neighboring tone
   Escape tone
   Anticipation
   Accented passing tone
   Accented neighboring tone
   Suspension (9–8, 7–6, 4–3, 2–3)

2. For definitions of the nonharmonic tones played in this section, consult your theory text.

3. A sound pattern is a three-note series of pitches, with the nonharmonic tone in the middle. The *sound pattern* of each nonharmonic tone is especially helpful in ear training.

4. Some items that are common to all of the above-listed nonharmonic tones:
   a. The nonharmonic tone is always *dissonant* (9th, 7th, 4th, 2nd).
   b. The nonharmonic tone is always the *middle* note of the pattern.
   c. The two notes on either side are always *consonant*.

5. One nonharmonic tone can be distinguished from another by the pattern of movement—by (S)tep, by (L)eap, or by (R)epeated pitch. The pattern of movement helps to distinguish among all of the above-listed nonharmonic tones except the passing tone and the neighboring tone.

6. Passing tones and neighboring tones can be distinguished only by the direction of the movement—

   Passing tone   = down-down or up-up

   Neighboring tone = up-down or down-up

7. The following example illustrates nonharmonic tones in a one-voice setting. Note that in all instances (1) the nonharmonic tone is dissonant, (2) the nonharmonic tone is the middle note, and (3) the first and third notes are consonant.

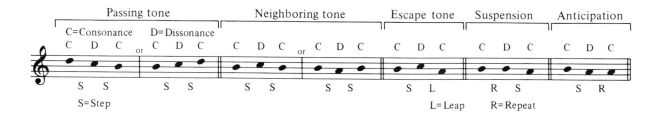

8. Practice playing these patterns until you know them thoroughly.

9. Before playing the two-voice illustrations, your instructor will play some of the one-voice examples to help acquaint you with the distinguishing characteristics of each nonharmonic tone type.

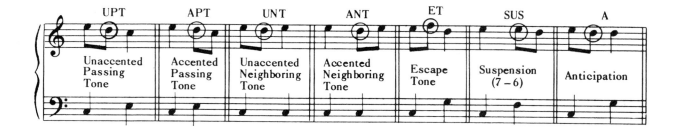

Circle the correct nonharmonic tone abbreviation:

Examples of the nonharmonic tones:

Nonharmonic tones are in the upper voice:

1. UPT   APT   UNT   ANT   ET   SUS   A   6. UPT   APT   UNT   ANT   ET   SUS   A

2. UPT   APT   UNT   ANT   ET   SUS   A   7. UPT   APT   UNT   ANT   ET   SUS   A

3. UPT   APT   UNT   ANT   ET   SUS   A   8. UPT   APT   UNT   ANT   ET   SUS   A

4. UPT   APT   UNT   ANT   ET   SUS   A   9. UPT   APT   UNT   ANT   ET   SUS   A

5. UPT   APT   UNT   ANT   ET   SUS   A   10. UPT   APT   UNT   ANT   ET   SUS   A

Nonharmonic tones are in the lower voice:

11. UPT   APT   UNT   ANT   ET   SUS   A   16. UPT   APT   UNT   ANT   ET   SUS   A

12. UPT   APT   UNT   ANT   ET   SUS   A   17. UPT   APT   UNT   ANT   ET   SUS   A

13. UPT   APT   UNT   ANT   ET   SUS   A   18. UPT   APT   UNT   ANT   ET   SUS   A

14. UPT   APT   UNT   ANT   ET   SUS   A   19. UPT   APT   UNT   ANT   ET   SUS   A

15. UPT   APT   UNT   ANT   ET   SUS   A   20. UPT   APT   UNT   ANT   ET   SUS   A

Nonharmonic tones may be in either voice:

21. UPT   APT   UNT   ANT   ET   SUS   A   26. UPT   APT   UNT   ANT   ET   SUS   A

22. UPT   APT   UNT   ANT   ET   SUS   A   27. UPT   APT   UNT   ANT   ET   SUS   A

23. UPT   APT   UNT   ANT   ET   SUS   A   28. UPT   APT   UNT   ANT   ET   SUS   A

24. UPT   APT   UNT   ANT   ET   SUS   A   29. UPT   APT   UNT   ANT   ET   SUS   A

25. UPT   APT   UNT   ANT   ET   SUS   A   30. UPT   APT   UNT   ANT   ET   SUS   A

L. ET Harmonic Function: I(i), ii(ii°), iii(III,III⁺), IV(iv), V, and vi(VI) Triads and Inversions

Each exercise consists of a series of four chords in block harmony.

In the blanks provided, write the analysis of each of the four chords.

Numbers 1–10 contain root-position triads only:

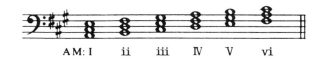

AM: I   ii   iii   IV   V   vi

1.–10. (R)

1. _____ _____ _____ _____   6. _____ _____ _____ _____

2. _____ _____ _____ _____   7. _____ _____ _____ _____

3. _____ _____ _____ _____   8. _____ _____ _____ _____

4. _____ _____ _____ _____   9. _____ _____ _____ _____

5. _____ _____ _____ _____   10. _____ _____ _____ _____

am: i   i⁶   ii°⁶   III   III⁶   III⁺   III⁺⁶   iv   iv⁶   V   V⁶   VI   VI⁶

Numbers 11–20 contain inversions:

11. _____ _____ _____ _____   16. _____ _____ _____ _____

12. _____ _____ _____ _____   17. _____ _____ _____ _____

13. _____ _____ _____ _____   18. _____ _____ _____ _____

14. _____ _____ _____ _____   19. _____ _____ _____ _____

15. _____ _____ _____ _____   20. _____ _____ _____ _____

8

A. SS Rhythm: Further Practice of Quarter-Beat Values

I

Procedure

1. Consider each measure as a module to be practiced separately or as part of a series requested by your instructor.
2. Follow procedures given in Unit 2, Section A, page 23. Work continually for both accuracy and speed—with accuracy taking precedence.

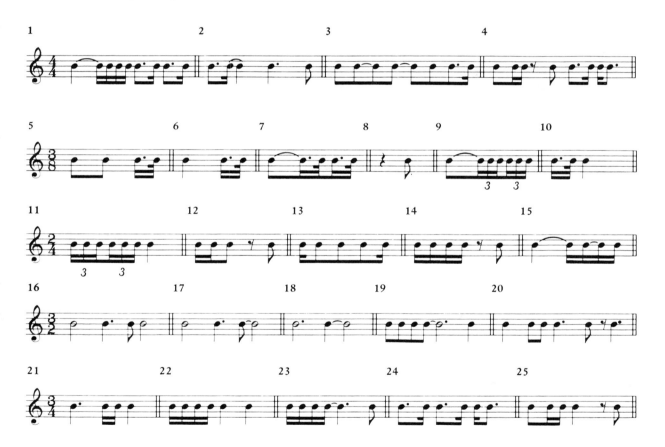

II Review of Compound Meter

Directions are the same as for Unit 5, Section A, page 87.

B. ET Rhythmic Dictation: Quarter-Beat Values

Each exercise consists of a two-measure melody.

Complete each rhythm on a neutral pitch.

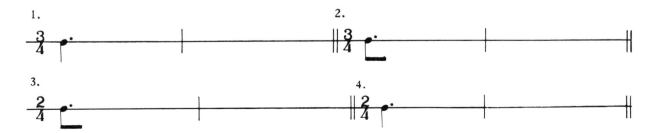

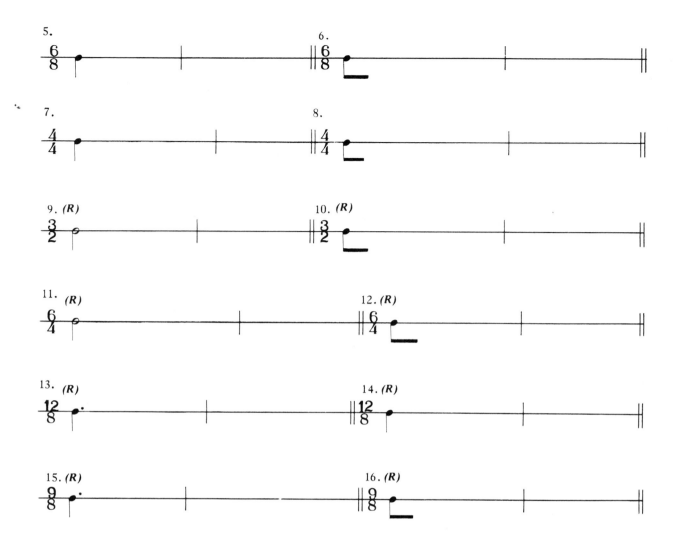

C. SS Diatonic Models for Interval Study
New Interval: M7
Review: m7

I

Exercises emphasizing the major 7th (M7).

The exercises in this section relate to the music of Verdi, Stravinsky, Wagner, Bach, and Beethoven—as represented in Section D (page 169) of this unit.

Exercises 1–9

The first nine exercises emphasize the minor 7th (F up to E♭ or E♭ down to F). Some familiar patterns, such as the passing-tone figure, chordal skip, and neighboring tones, are review material from previous units. Two neighboring-tone figures are combined to form a *double neighboring tone* (also known as *changing tones*).

Exercises 1–5 pertain to the first Bach fragment (Section D, page 169) and exercises 6–9 to the Wagner fragments (Section D, numbers 2, 3, and 4).

Follow the same procedure as in previous units (see Units 1 and 2, Section C). For extra practice, sing exercise 5 in keys a minor 3rd above (i.e., c, e♭, f♯), then sing exercise 9 in keys a minor 3rd below (E♭, C, A, etc.). This is a version of tossing triads and antiphonal singing, but requires even more concentration. See the following model:

If you find it difficult to sing exercise 9 in keys separated by a minor 3rd (E♭, C, A), the reason is that the melodic patterns form part of an octatonic scale (i.e., a scale of alternating major and minor seconds). The tonal relationships studied thus far are considerably different in the octatonic scale. See the following model:

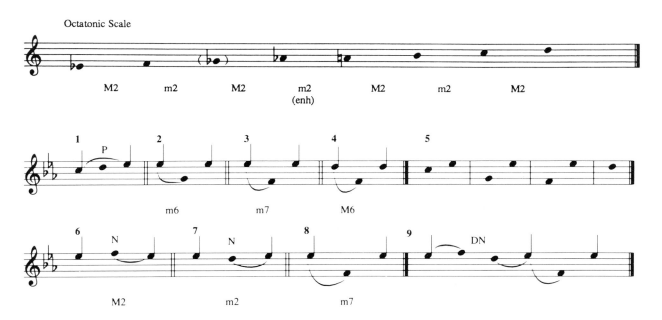

If you experience difficulty with exercise 9, fill in the minor 7th as follows:

Exercises 10–11

Only two exercises are needed to introduce the major 7th (M7) from E♭ to D. These are preparatory materials for melodic fragments 5–7 (Section D, page 169–170).

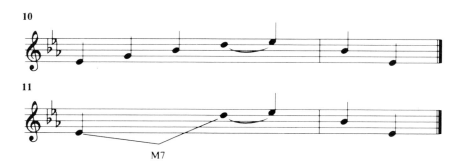

Exercises 12–13

Only two exercises are necessary to introduce the M7th (from A♭ to G) as preparation for melodic fragments 8 and 9, page 170. Exercise 13 is almost the reverse of no. 12. Tossing these exercises might exceed the stress limit of nearby windows and is therefore not recommended by the authors.

Exercises 14–15

These are quite similar to numbers 10 and 11, except that they are in minor keys. For those of you who wish to emphasize *relative* relationship, C minor is provided, and for others who prefer *parallel* relationship, e♭ (E-flat minor) is available.

It would be helpful to practice 10–11 and 14–15 in combination. Numbers 10 and 11 are preparation for melodic fragments 10, 10a, 11, and 11a (Section D, page 170).

Fragments 12, 12a, 13, and 13a in Section D rely on your proficiency in recognizing scale lines. No additional exercises are needed.

II Alto Clef*

Return now to the familiar diatonic models for Unit 4, Section C (page 70) for practice in clef reading. In numbers 1–30, to verify your versatility, substitute the alto clef for the given clef and change the key signature. See the following model:

Starting in Unit 9, some exercises will be given in alto and tenor clefs.

D. SS Melodic Fragments for Interval Singing
New Interval: M7
Review: m7

E. ET Models and Embellishments: Cadence Formulas in Two Voices

1. The four models in this section are based on two-voice authentic cadences. Sing both parts of these structures before class.
2. Your instructor will play the structure followed by embellishments of that structure.
3. Write the embellishments on the numbered staves provided below each model.

F. SS Melodies for Review and Practice in Singing at Performance Tempo

1. All melodies are intended to be sung at performance tempo on the first attempt.
2. Melodies 1–3 are from Verdi's opera *Nabucco*. Melodies 4–10 are folk songs. A five-second scan before singing is encouraged. Try to "imagine" the sound of each pitch.
3. Melodies 11–20 are shorter prepared exercises designed to be sung *without* prior scanning of any kind.

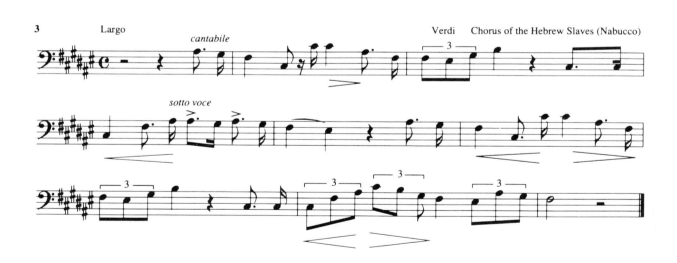

G. ET Melodic Dictation: Two-Phrase Melodies

Each exercise is a melody composed of two phrases. The second phrase begins immediately after the caesura, ||, marked in each melody.

1. Complete each melody on the staff in notation. The first note(s) of each phrase is (are) given.
2. As you hear the melody, try to memorize each phrase so that you can sing it accurately in your mind.
3. Think of the scale degree each pitch represents by including solfeggio syllables or numbers.
4. When all pitches are accounted for, you are ready to write the phrase on the staff.

*(R) means recorded.

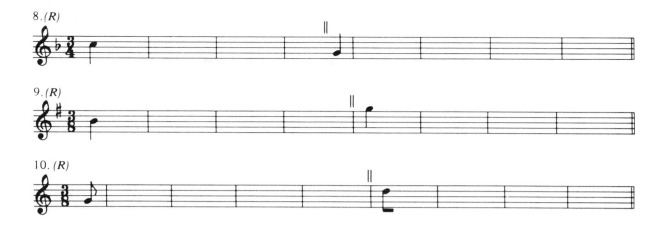

H. SS Melodies for Careful Study and Preparation

Procedure for Completing Each Melody

1. Some melodies here contain an occasional major or minor 7th interval. Thus, it is suggested that Section D of Unit 7 be studied either before or simultaneously with this material.
2. For interval practice, select a melody and read through it (without singing), naming the intervals as you read. Try to increase the speed of interval identification as much as you can without sacrificing accuracy.
3. Then return to the beginning of the melody and sing it with the solfeggio or number system preferred by your instructor.

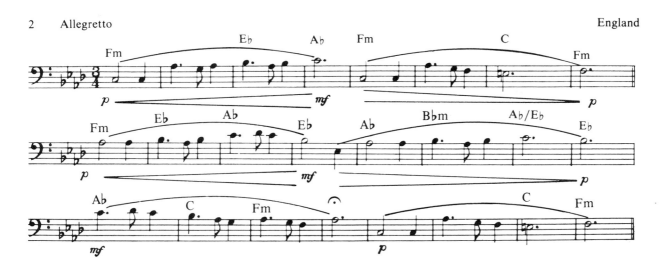

2   Allegretto   England

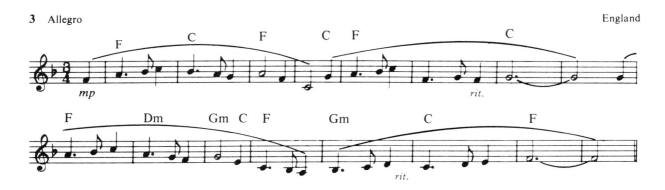

3   Allegro   England

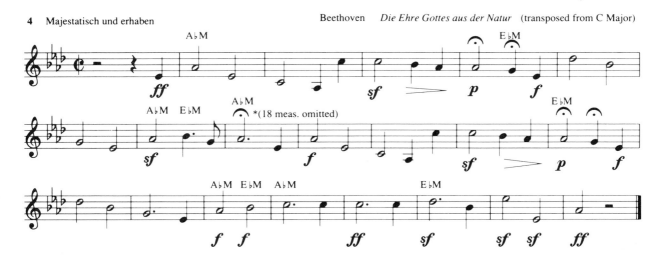

4   **Majestatisch und erhaben**   Beethoven   *Die Ehre Gottes aus der Natur*   (transposed from C Major)

9 ♩ – 104   Pachelbel

10 ♩ – 160   Bull   *The King's Hunting Jigg*

11 ♩ – 66   Kuhnau

12   Moderato   Anonymous   *God for Poland*

13 Andante

14 Andante con Moto

Spain

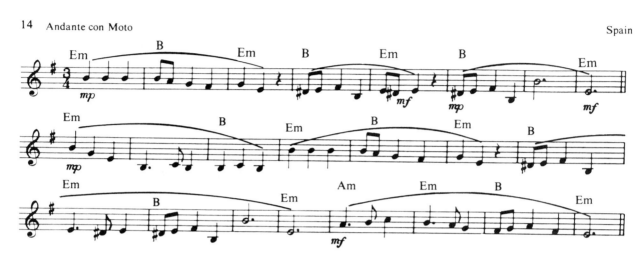

15 Allegretto

Denmark

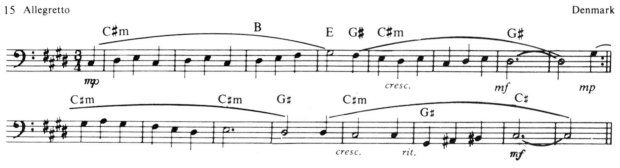

16 ♩ – 92

Schubert

25 ♩ – 88

Buxtehude

26 Marchlike

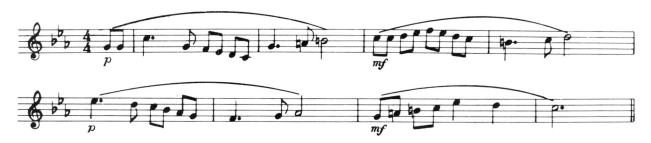

27 Turgid

28 Andante

30   Bach   Art of the Fugue, Contrapunctus XIII (Rectus)

Contrapunctus XIII (Inversus) (two octaves lower)

31

I. ET New Intervals: m7 and M7

Intervals studied to date: m2, M2, m3, M3, P4, P5, m6, M6

Each exercise consists of a single interval. The first note is given.

1.   Write the second note of the interval on the staff.
2.   Place the name of the interval in the blank provided.
3.   The best way to identify both the major and minor 7th is to practice singing them above and below a variety of given pitches. Soon you will have them well in mind and can recognize their peculiar qualities without having to rely on a special system.

4. Another method, of short-term benefit, is to think of major and minor 7ths as inversions of minor or major 2nds—easier to identify. Sing an octave above or below (depending on the situation) to get into proper range. Then, sing up or down a half- or whole-step to complete the original major or minor 7th.

The missing note is above the given note:

11.–30. (R)

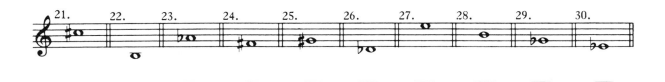

The missing note is below the given note:

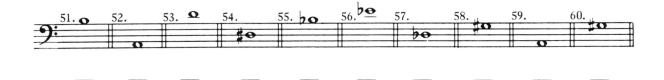

J. SS Ensemble Excerpts: Two, Three, and Four Voices

Procedure

Follow procedures outlined in Unit 3, Section J, page 61.

1   A. Scarlatti

2   Folk Song   *Charlie, My Darlin'*

3

Bach

4

Haydn

5

Bach   Contrapunctus V (Art of the Fugue)

6 Allegretto

Beethoven   WoO50, II

*See Unit 9 C and D for d5.

7 ♩ - 88

Canon at the Octave

8 ♩ – 69 – 92   Free Imitation

K. ET Harmonic Dictation: I(i), ii, IV(iv), and V Triads in Four-Part Chorale Phrases

Each exercise consists of a phrase from a chorale. Numbers 7–14 were harmonized by Bach.

1.	Numbers	Harmonic Vocabulary	Triad Positions	Nonharmonic Tones
	1–6	I (i), ii, V	All root position	UPT and 4–3 SUS only
	7–9	I (i) and V only	Root position and 1st inversion	UPT, APT, and 2–3 SUS
	10–14	I (i), IV (iv), and V only	Root position, 1st inversion, and 2nd inversion	UPT, LNT, and 4–3 SUS
	15–16	I, ii, IV, and V	Root position and 1st inversion	UPT only

2. Indicate the roman-numeral analysis of each triad in the blanks provided.
3. List nonharmonic tones beneath the harmonic analysis.
4. If the instructor requests it, give the melodic line of both the soprano and bass voices.
5. If the instructor requests it, give the melodic line of both the alto and tenor voices.

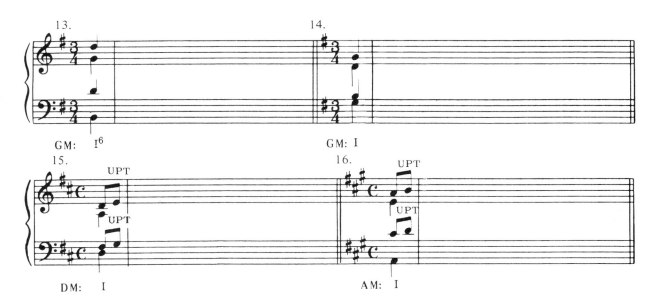

L. ET Harmonic Function: Diatonic Triads (Major Mode)

Each exercise consists of four chords in block harmony.

Write the roman-numeral analysis of each chord in the blank provided.

Numbers 1–15 use I, ii, iii, IV, V, vi

Numbers 1–15 contain root-position triads only:

1.–10. (R)

1. _____ _____ _____ _____   9. _____ _____ _____ _____

2. _____ _____ _____ _____   10. _____ _____ _____ _____

3. _____ _____ _____ _____   11. _____ _____ _____ _____

4. _____ _____ _____ _____   12. _____ _____ _____ _____

5. _____ _____ _____ _____   13. _____ _____ _____ _____

6. _____ _____ _____ _____   14. _____ _____ _____ _____

7. _____ _____ _____ _____   15. _____ _____ _____ _____

8. _____ _____ _____ _____

Numbers 16–25 contain   I, ii, iii, IV, V, vi
                          I^6, ii^6, iii^6, IV^6, V^6, vi^6, $vii°^6$

F M: I   I6   ii   ii 6   iii   iii 6   IV   IV6   V   V6   vi   vi 6   vii o 6

Numbers 16–25 contain inversions:

16. _____ _____ _____ _____   21. _____ _____ _____ _____

17. _____ _____ _____ _____   22. _____ _____ _____ _____

18. _____ _____ _____ _____   23 _____ _____ _____ _____

19. _____ _____ _____ _____   24. _____ _____ _____ _____

20. _____ _____ _____ _____   25. _____ _____ _____ _____

‡Challenging example.

9

A. SS Rhythm: Subdivisions of the Beat in Compound Meters

I: Duple Subdivisions in Compound Meters

1. Consider each measure as a module to be practiced separately, or as part of a series requested by your instructor.
2. Follow procedures given in Unit 2, Section A, page 23. Work continually for both accuracy and speed—with accuracy taking precedence.

Quarter-beat values in compound meter:

After completing these rhythm exercises as suggested at the beginning of the section, ask half the class to clap or say a line forward while the other half reads the same line backward from end to beginning. To create a different quality of sound for each section, have the second group drum on their chairs with the palms of their hands.

II: Triple Subdivisions in Simple and Compound Meters

Sing the following exercises on a neutral pitch:

1. Clap the meter.
   Say the rhythm using rhythm syllables.
2. Say the meter using numbers.
   Clap the rhythm.
3. Tap the meter with one hand.
   Tap the rhythm with the other hand.
4. Half the class taps the meter.
   The other half taps the rhythm.

1

2   Rhythmic Crescendo and Decrescendo

3

4

5

B. ET Rhythmic Dictation: Compound Meters with Quarter-Beat Values

Each exercise is a short, two-measure melodic excerpt. The meter signature and beginning durational value are given.

Complete each rhythm on a neutral pitch.

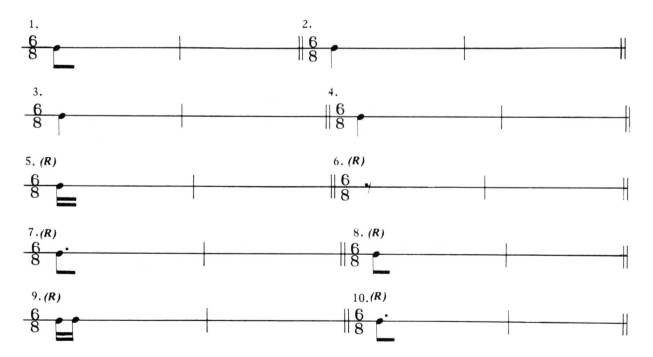

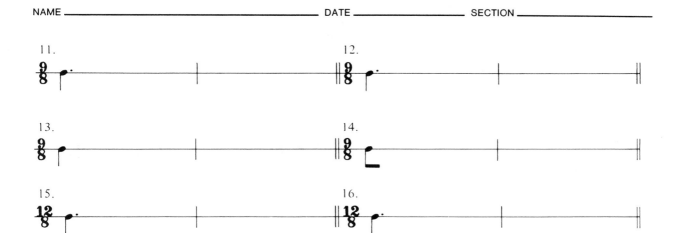

C. SS Diatonic and Chromatic Models for Interval Study
New Intervals: A4, d5

I

Emphasis on the tritone (A4 or d5).

The models in this section relate to the melodic fragments of Bach, Beethoven, and Mozart (see Section D, page 20). The following chart shows in detail the relationships between models and fragments:

Use procedures described in Unit 1, Section C (page 6).

Exercises 1–5

These emphasize the resolution of the d5th (D♯–A) to the M3rd (E–G♯), as given in the following model:

Models	Fragments
1 & 2	1
2	2
3	3
4	4
5	5
6	6
7 a & b	7 a & b
8 a & b	8 a & b
9 a & b	9 a & b
10 a & b	10 a & b
11 a & b	11 a & b
12 a & b	12 a & b

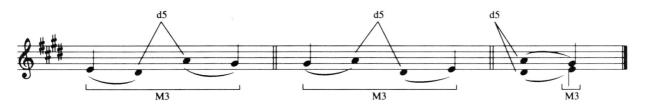

Learning to sing the exercises derived from this excerpt will help you understand the intricacies of voice leading involved in the treatment of tritones. Most often successive melodic tritones are harmonized by dominant 7th chords, moving sequentially downward by P5ths.

For further study, sing exercise 2 in all major keys, transposing to each new key by perfect 5ths down or perfect 4ths up. Please see the following model:

If you can stand the dizzying speed, try the following accelerated method for traveling through the various keys:

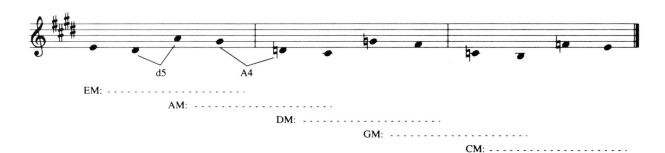

Exercise 6

This model shows the resolution of the A4 (F♯—B♯) to the M6 (E—C♯).

Exercises 7–12

For those of you who are learning la-based minor, sing 7a–12a. If your instructor prefers do-based minor, sing 7b–12b. If fixed la or chromatic fixed do is the preference, you should sing both types of models (7a–12b). Some of the intervals introduced in this unit are marked on the score but are not labeled. Make sure you can quickly identify each.

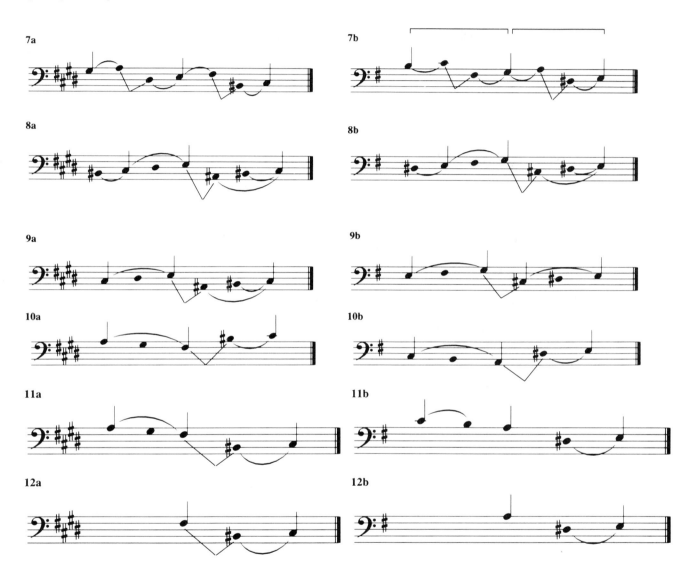

II: Alto and Tenor Clefs

Alto Clef*

Return to the familiar diatonic models of Unit 5, Section C for practice in reading the alto clef. In numbers 1–36, substitute the alto clef for the treble clef and change the key signature. See the following illustration:

Tenor Clef*

For practice in reading the tenor clef, go back to Unit 1, Section C. In numbers 1–26, substitute the tenor clef for the treble and change the key signature. See the following illustration:

D. SS Melodic Fragments for Interval Singing
New Intervals: A4, d5

(Note to the Instructor: Relate these melodies to models found in Section C, page 197.)

Sing each melody at the tempo indicated:

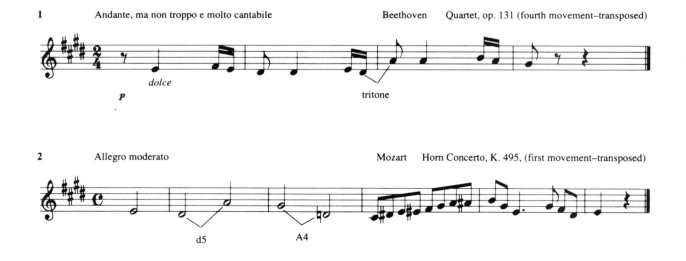

3   Alla danza tedesca   Beethoven   Quartet, op. 130, (fourth movement–transposed)

d5

4   Rondo   Mozart   Horn Concerto, K. 417, (third movement–transposed)

d5

5   Più lento   Beethoven   Quartet, op. 135 (third movement)

d5

6   Allegro   Beethoven   op.131, no. 7

A4

7   a   b   Bach   Chorale no. 78 (abridged and transposed)

c♯m: d5   d5   em: d5   d5

8   a   b   Bach   Chorale no. 126 (transposed)

d5   d5

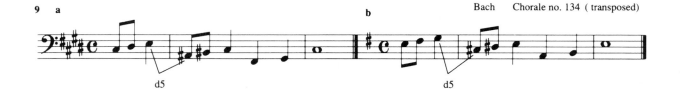

9 a   b   Bach   Chorale no. 134 (transposed)

d5   d5

10 a   b   Bach   Chorale no. 170 (transposed)

A4   A4

11 a   b   Bach   Chorale no. 178 (transposed)

d5   d5

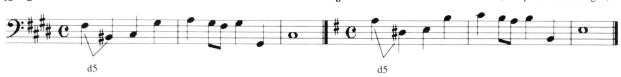

12 a   b   Bach   Chorale no. 172 (transposed and abridged)

d5   d5

Supplemental Fragments emphasizing secondary leading-tone [LT] functions.

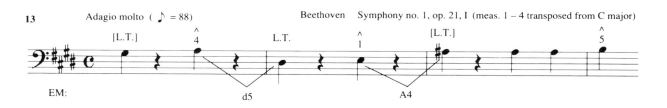

13   Adagio molto (♪ = 88)   Beethoven   Symphony no. 1, op. 21, I (meas. 1 – 4 transposed from C major)

[L.T.] $\hat{4}$ L.T. $\hat{1}$ [L.T.] $\hat{5}$

EM: d5   A4

14   Allegro con brio (♩ = 112)   Beethoven   Symphony no. 1, op. 21 (meas. 41 – 45 abridged and transposed)

L.T. $\hat{1}$ [L.T.] $\hat{2}$ [L.T.] $\hat{3}$ L.T. $\hat{4}$ [L.T.] $\hat{5}$

EM:

E. ET Models and Embellishments:
Chord Progression with Melodic Embellishments

1. The model in this section is made up of a famous chord progression with melodic and textural embellishments. You will probably recognize it as the progression of the Pachelbel "Canon." Sing all parts of this structure before class.
2. Your instructor will play the structure followed by embellishments of that structure.
3. Write the model's embellishments on the numbered staves provided.

Embellishments:

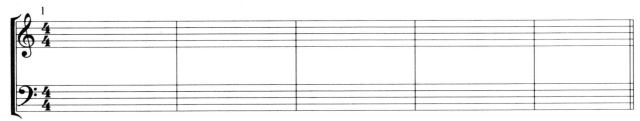

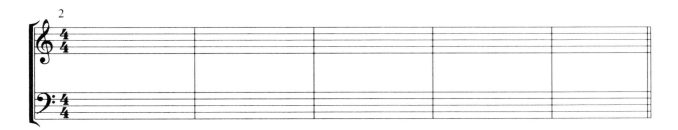

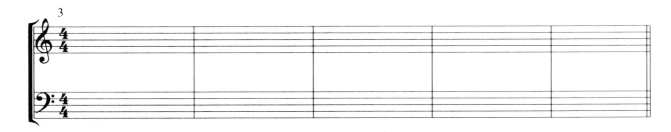

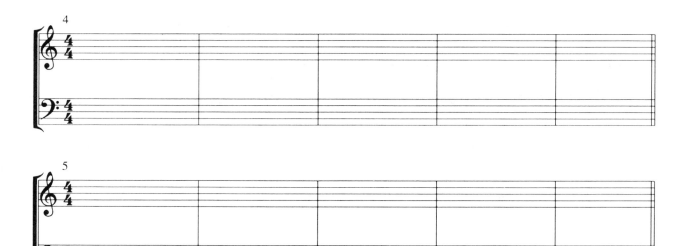

F. SS Melodies for Practice in Speed Singing

Procedure for Completing Each Melody

1. Tempo markings are given for the melodies below.
2. Since the melodies are slightly more difficult rhythmically, read each through first using rhythm syllables.
3. Practice singing each as fast as possible without error.

G. ET Melodic Dictation: Melodies with Larger Leaps

Each exercise consists of a short, two-measure melody.

Complete each melody on the staff in notation. The first note of each melody is given.

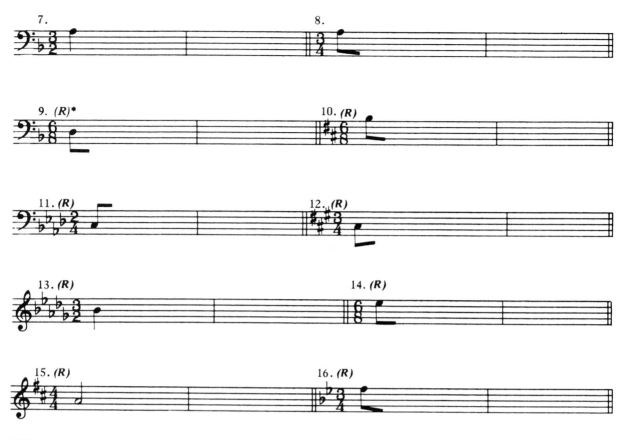

*(R) means recorded.

H. SS Melodies for Careful Study: Chromatic Alterations, Modulating, and Nonmodulating

I

1. The melodies in this part contain modulations and are excerpted from instrumental music.
2. The following are some suggestions for singing the melodies in this part.
   a. Before singing, scan each melody carefully to determine where the modulation begins.
   b. The introduction of an accidental is one clue to a modulation. As in no. 1 (below), a C♯ appears in measure 13 and occurs three more times before the end of the excerpt. Remember that adding a C♯ to the signature (F♯) would render D major—or possibly B minor.
   c. Examine phrase endings to determine implied cadences in a different key. Again in no. 1 (below) the final melodic cadence consists of C♯ to D. Along with the evidence from (b) above, the key of D major is strongly suggested.
   d. Sometimes in modulations from a major key to its relative minor, or vice-versa, telltale accidentals are nonexistent.
   e. Looking for strong dominant-tonic relationships in a melody is also helpful in spotting modulations. In measures 13–21 of no. 1 (below) the new tonic note (D) and its dominant (A) are both prominent.

f. Almost all of the melodies in this text are excerpted from a harmonic texture that is, of course,
deleted. Thus, occasionally, modulation indicators are not present in the melody itself, and changes
of key are extremely difficult to determine. Number 5 (by Liszt) offers only a slight clue to the
modulation—two B naturals in the last four measures.

5 Allegretto Pastorale   Liszt   Les Preludes

6   Couperin   *Sweet Charms*

7 Dvorak   Slavonic Dance, op. 46, no. 1

8 Allegretto   Mozart Symphony no. 41, K. 551

9 Menuet   Haydn   Minuet

10 Moderato   Haydn   Sonatina, Hob. XVI: 1

II

1. The melodies in this part are extracted from compositions by Mozart.
2. Not all of the melodies contain modulations, but in addition to the possibility of modulations, melodies in this part may also include chromatic alterations due to one or another of the following:
   a. accompaniments with secondary dominant or leading-tone harmonies
   b. accompaniments with other chromatic harmonies such as borrowed chords, augmented 6ths, Neapolitan 6ths, etc.
   c. chromatic nonharmonic tones
3. Your instructor will provide directions for the use of syllables or numbers as they relate to the sources of alteration listed above.

3 Larghetto   Mozart *Life's Journey*

4 Calmato   Mozart *Contentment*

5 Giocoso   Mozart *Longing for Spring*

*See Unit 13 C and D for d₄.

9 No tempo given   Mozart *No More Than That Tell You*

10 Andante   Mozart *Evening Song*

I. ET Interval: The Tritone

Intervals studied to date: m2, M2, m3, P4, P5, m6, M6, m7, M7

Each exercise consists of a single interval. The first note is given.

1. Write the second note of the interval on the staff.
2. Place the name of the interval in the blank provided.
3. The **tritone** (augmented 4th and diminished 5th) occurs in both major and harmonic minor from 4th to 7th scale degrees, but most musicians find it difficult to associate the sound with scales because melodic skips of a tritone are not very numerous.
4. The tritone occurs in the diminished triad as well, but it, too, is not as common as either the major or minor triad.
5. Imagine the sound of a P5th and diminish that interval by a half-step.

The second note is above the first:

11.–30. (R)

The second note is below the first:

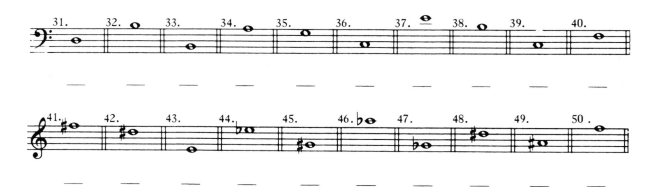

J. SS Ensemble Excerpts: Two, Three, and Four Voices

Procedure

Follow procedures outlined in Unit 3, Section J, page 61.

1

Folk Song   *Acres of Clams*

2

A. Scarlatti

Salieri

3

5 Andante

6 ♩ - 104   Canon at the Octave

7 ♩ - 104   Canon at the Octave

8 ♩ - 112

K. ET Harmonic Dictation: The I(i), ii(ii°), IV(iv), and V Triads in Four-Part Chorale Phrases

Phrases

Each exercise consists of a phrase from a **chorale.** Numbers 7–16 were harmonized by Bach. The harmonic vocabulary is as follows:

Numbers 1–6:   All triads are in root position.

Numbers 7–16:   Triads are in inversion as well as root position.

1. Indicate the roman-numeral analysis of each triad in the blanks provided.
2. List any nonharmonic tones beneath the harmonic analysis.
3. If the instructor requests it, give the melodic line of both the soprano and bass voices.
4. If the instructor requests it, give the melodic line of both the alto and tenor voices.

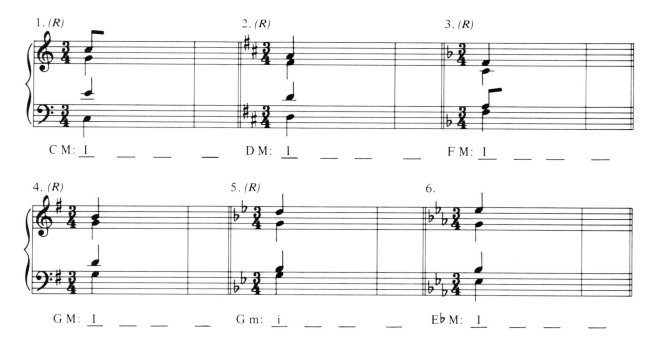

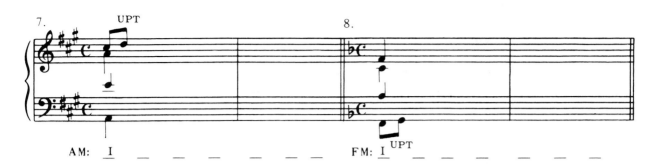

7. UPT

A M: I _ _ _ _ _

8. FM: I UPT

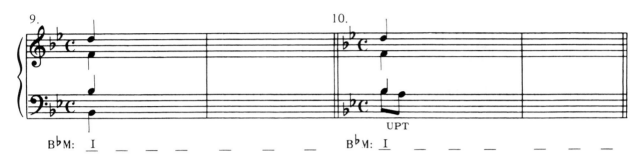

9. B♭M: I _ _ _ _ _

10. B♭M: I _ _ _ _ _
UPT

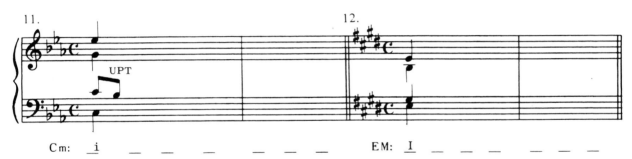

11. UPT

Cm: i _ _ _ _ _

12. EM: I _ _ _ _ _

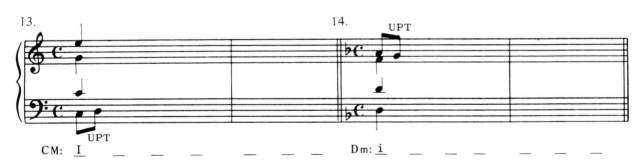

13. UPT

CM: I _ _ _ _ _
UPT

14. UPT

Dm: i _ _ _ _ _

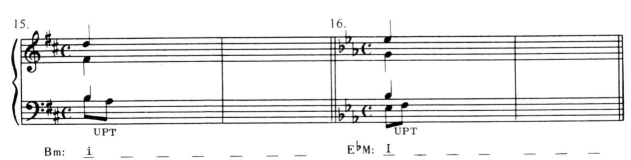

15. Bm: i _ _ _ _ _
UPT

16. E♭M: I _ _ _ _ _
UPT

L. ET Harmonic Function: Dominant 7th Chord and Inversions

Each exercise consists of a series of four chords in block harmony.

1. Analyze each of the four chords in the blanks provided.
2. The V^7 is the only new chord introduced in this unit. It is analyzed as follows:

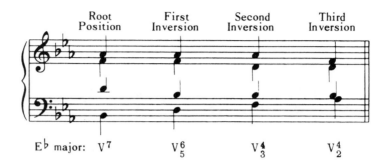

3. Write the analysis in the blanks provided.
Numbers 1–15 contain root-position chords only:

1.–10. (R)

1. _____ _____ _____ _____
2. _____ _____ _____ _____
3. _____ _____ _____ _____
4. _____ _____ _____ _____
5. _____ _____ _____ _____
6. _____ _____ _____ _____
7. _____ _____ _____ _____
8. _____ _____ _____ _____

9. _____ _____ _____ _____
10. _____ _____ _____ _____
11. _____ _____ _____ _____
12. _____ _____ _____ _____
13. _____ _____ _____ _____
14. _____ _____ _____ _____
15. _____ _____ _____ _____

Numbers 16–25 contain inversions:

16. _____ _____ _____ _____
17. _____ _____ _____ _____
18. _____ _____ _____ _____
19. _____ _____ _____ _____
20. _____ _____ _____ _____

21. _____ _____ _____ _____
22. _____ _____ _____ _____
23. _____ _____ _____ _____
24. _____ _____ _____ _____
25. _____ _____ _____ _____

·····10·····

A. SS Rhythm: Triplets and Mixed Meters

I: Procedure

1. Consider each measure as a module to be practiced separately, or as part of a series requested by your instructor.
2. Follow procedures given in Unit 2, Section A, page 23. Work continually for both accuracy and speed—with accuracy taking precedence.

II: Triplets

B. ET Rhythmic Dictation: Triple and Triplet Subdivisions

Each exercise consists of a short melodic excerpt of music. Most, but not all of these exercises contain triple or triplet subdivision of the beat.

Complete the rhythm of each excerpt on a neutral pitch.

1.

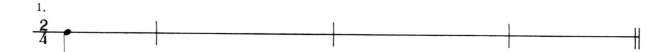

2.

3.

4.

5. *(R)*

These rhythms are a review of previous material.

6. *(R)*

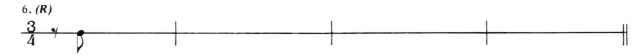

7. *(R)*

8. *(R)*

C. SS Diatonic and Chromatic Models for Interval Study Review: A4, d5

I

Emphasis on intervals of the augmented 4th and diminished 5th

As in Section C of Unit 9, these exercises focus on the tritone. But in this unit, the models are based on fragments by a different set of composers: Wagner, Stravinsky, Berg, Franck, Moussorgsky, Debussy, Schubert, and Barber (see Section D, page 228). Many of these models are extracted from highly chromatic textures, but the exercises themselves are, for the most part, diatonic. Often the notes of resolution associated with the tritone, in traditional terms, are partially or fully absent in some exercises.

The unifying thread that runs throughout Sections C and D of this unit is the pitch-specific nature of the tritone D♯ and A. The one exception occurs in melodic fragments 9–11, where the transposition to parallel minor changes D♯–A to F♯–C.

The following table indicates how the models (this section) relate to the fragments (Section D).

Models	Fragments
1 & 2	1 & 2
3	3
4	2
5	4
6	6
7	5
8	7
9	8
10	9
11	10
12	11

Exercises 1–3

Follow the same procedure as in previous units. For extra practice, sing exercises 1 and 2 in all major keys. You might try tossing tritones at each other using the following model:

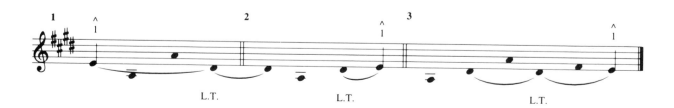

Exercises 4–6

Exercise 4 shows how a tritone (A–D♯) is filled in with a major 3rd (A–C♯) and a major 2nd (C♯–D♯). Exercises 5 and 6 show another way of filling in the same tritone with a major 2nd (A–B) and a major 3rd (B–D♯).

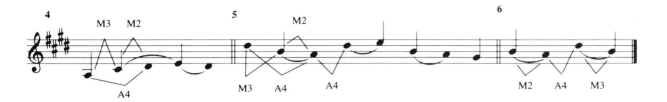

Exercises 7–9

These exercises feature a tritone that is not filled in.

Exercises 10–12

These models relate to fragments 9, 10, and 11 of Section D (page 230).

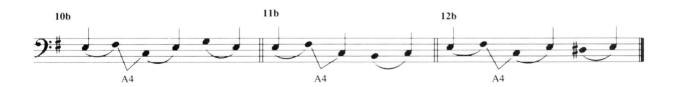

II: Alto and Tenor clefs

a. Alto clef*

Return now to the familiar diatonic models of Unit 6, Section C for practice in reading the alto clef. In numbers 1–24, substitute the alto clef for the given clef and change the key signature.

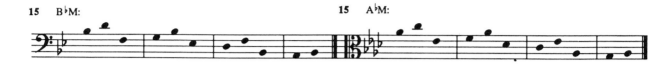

b. Tenor clef*

Return to the diatonic models of Unit 2, Section C for practice in reading the tenor clef. In numbers 1–39, substitute the tenor clef for the treble clef and change the key signature.

D. SS Melodic Fragments for Interval Singing Review: A4, d5

(Note to the instructor: Relate these fragments to Section C of this unit.)

Sing each fragment as written. Most new intervals are labeled.

"I Hear An Army" Music by Samuel Barber. Copyright © 1939 (Renewed) G. Schirmer, Inc. International Copyright Secured. All Rights Reserved. Used by permission.

3 Lento cantabile

Stravinsky Petroushka, Third Tableau (transposed)

A4   d5   d5

© Copyright by Edition Russe de Musique. Copyright assigned to Boosey & Hawkes, Inc. Revised edition © Copyright 1947, 1948 by Boosey & Hawkes, Inc.; Copyright Renewed. Reprinted by permission of Boosey & Hawkes, Inc.

4 Poco a poco sempre - più - come una pastorale

Berg   Violin Concerto, I A Carinthian Folk Tune (transposed)

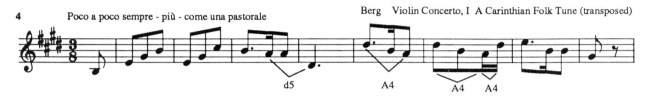

d5   A4   A4   A4

Berg *Violin Concerto* Copyright 1938 by Universal Edition. Copyright Renewed. All Rights Reserved. Used by permission of European American Music Distributors Corporation, sole U.S. and Canadian agent for Universal Edition.

5 Feierlich

Wagner The Twilight of the Gods, Act III, Scene III

A4   A4

6 Allegro

Franck Violin Sonata for Violin and Piano (second movement–transposed)

A4

Debussy Ballades of François Villon (transposed)

7 Expressif et moqueur

A4

8   Feierlich   Wagner The Twilight of the Gods, Act III, Scene III (transposed)

d5

9   **A**   **B** Moussorgsky *Boris Godounov,* Act I, Scene I (transposed)

Andante tranquillo

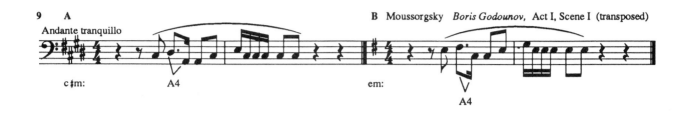

c♯m: A4   em: A4

10   **A**   **B**   Schubert   *Ihr Bild* (Her Picture) (transposed)

Langsam

c♯m: A4   em: A4

11   **A**   Moderato   **B**   Barber   "Rain Has Fallen" (transposed)

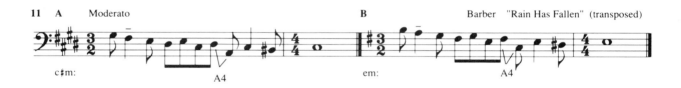

c♯m: A4   em: A4

E. ET Models and Embellishments: I-V-I Progression with Diatonic Melodic Embellishments

1. The model in this section is a I-V-I progression using four voices. The upper three voices are always in open position. Sing all parts of this structure before class.
2. Your instructor will play the structure followed by embellishments of that structure.
3. Write the model's embellishments on the numbered staves provided.

Model: Embellishments:

Two five-measure examples based on the same model.

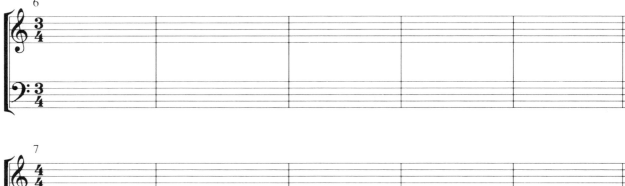

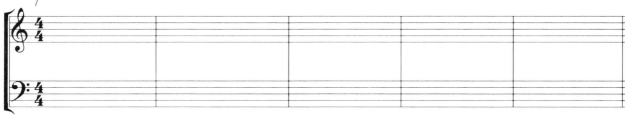

F. SS Melodies for Review and Practice in Singing at Performance Tempo

Procedure for Completing Each Melody

1. The goal of this section is to sing each melody with accuracy at performance tempo on the *first* attempt.
2. Before singing, scan each melody, silently trying to imagine the sound of each note.
3. When satisfied that the melody is well in mind, you are ready to sing.

3 Allegretto · Purcell · *Mad Bess* From Orpheus Britannicus

4 Andante espressivo · Franz · *Dedication*, op. 14, no. 1

5 Allegretto · Chopin *The Parted Lovers*

6 Nicht zu geschwind, doch Kräftig · Schubert · *My Abode*, Schwanengesang, no. 5

7 Con Spirito · Purcell · *Man is for the Woman Made* From Orpheus Britannicus

G. ET Melodic Dictation: Short Melodies from Music Literature

Each exercise consists of a short melodic excerpt from music literature.

Complete each melody on the staff in notation.

7.   8. *(R)*

9. *(R)**   10. *(R)*

11. *(R)*   12. *(R)*

13. *(R)*   14. *(R)*

*(R) means recorded.

H. SS Melodies for Careful Study and Preparation:
Chromatic Alterations, Modulating

1. All of the melodies in this section are taken from works by Felix Mendelssohn (Songs Without Words), Clara Schumann, Robert Schumann, and George Frideric Handel.
2. All include alterations due to one or another of the following:
   a. accompaniments with secondary-dominant or leading-tone harmonies
   b. accompaniments with other chromatic harmonies such as borrowed chords augmented 6ths, Neapolitan 6ths, and so on.
   c. fully established modulations
   d. chromatic nonharmonic tones
3. Your instructor will provide directions for the use of syllables or numbers as they relate to the sources of alteration listed above.

Mendelssohn op. 30/3 (abridged)

2   Allegretto tranquillo

cantabile

Transpose down a minor 3rd to
D major, using the soprano clef – starting note F♯

3   Allegro non troppo   Mendelssohn   op. 53/2 (abridged)

Transpose down a minor 3rd to C major, using the soprano clef.

4   Adagio cantabile   Mendelssohn   op. 53/4 (abridged)

5   Andante espressivo   Mendelssohn   Op. 62/1 (abridged)

6   Allegretto grazioso   Mendelssohn   Op. 62/6 (adapted and abridged)

7   Andante sostenuto   Mendelssohn   Op. 85/4 (abridged)

Transpose down a minor 3rd to B, using the soprano clef.

8   Adagio   Mendelssohn   Op. 102/2 (abridged)

9   Presto   Mendelssohn   Op. 102/3 (abridged)

Breitkopf & Härtl, Wiesbaden. Used by permission.

14   Im erzahlenden ton   Schumann

15   Munter

16   Sehr mässig   Schumann

17   Nicht schnell   Schumann

18   Nach und nach leidenschaftlicher   Schumann

19   Langsam   Schumann

20   Schnell   Schumann

21   Innig, lebhaft   Schumann

22   Handel   Chaconne in G Major, variation 9

23   Handel   Suite in D Minor, *Sarabande*

I. ET Intervals: All Intervals Played Harmonically

Each exercise consists of a single interval played harmonically.

1. Write the name of the interval in the blank provided.
2. Write the remaining note on the staff.

The given note is the lower of the two:

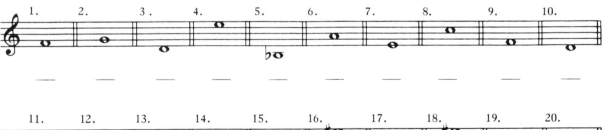

The given note is the upper of the two:

31.–60. (R)

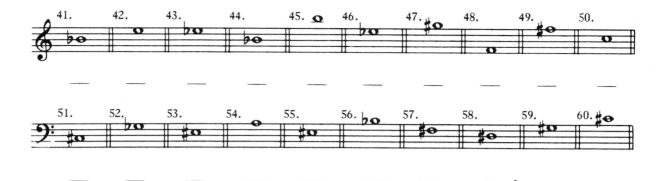

J. SS Ensemble Excerpts: Two, Three, and Four Voices

Procedure

Follow procedures outlined in Unit 3, Section J, page 61.

1

J. K. F. Fischer

2

Folk Song   *Sinner Man*

3

Beethoven

Number 4 of this section, written around 1420, is excerpted from a choral composition by Guillaume Dufay. Since the style is markedly different from that of other compositions in this unit, some timely observations are in order:

1. The absence of a key signature in the upper (alto) voice is typical of fifteenth-century practice.
2. The use of accidentals above the staves refers to *musica ficta*. These accidentals are placed there by modern-day editors to indicate that the original manuscript did not contain them, but singers of the period conventionally added them according to the common practice of the time. Such accidentals should be included as if they were to the left of the note.
3. Note the *Landini* cadence in measures 6–7 and 15–16. A Landini cadence is created when the sixth degree of the mode (last note in the upper voice, measure 6) is inserted between the leading tone and the final.
4. The double leading-tone progression (measures 3–4) in which the two upper voices progress by half steps is common to the period.
5. The "8" beneath the treble clefs in the lower (tenor) two voices indicates that these two voices should be sung an octave lower than printed.

Dufay

G. P. Telemann   Fuga 2

K. ET Harmonic Dictation: I(i), ii, IV(iv), V, vi(VI), and vii° Triads in Four-Part Chorale Phrases

Each exercise consists of a chorale phrase. The harmonic vocabulary is as follows:

Numbers	Harmony Included	Positions
1–6	All listed above	Root position exclusively
7–12	All listed above, except vi (VI) An occasional vii°	Root position and inversions

1. Indicate the roman-numeral analysis of each triad in the blanks provided.
2. List nonharmonic tones beneath the harmonic analysis.
3. If the instructor requests it, give the melodic line of both the soprano and bass voices.
4. If the instructor requests it, give the melodic line of both the alto and tenor voices.

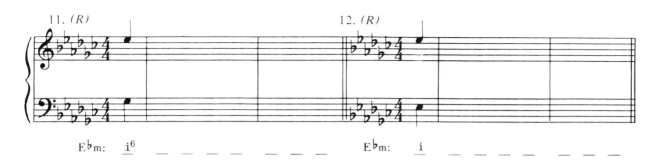

$E^{\flat}$m: $\underline{i^6}$ _ _ _ _ _ _ _ $E^{\flat}$m: $\underline{i}$ _ _ _ _ _ _ _

L. ET Harmonic Function: Nondominant 7th Chords

Each exercise consists of a series of four chords in block harmony.

Indicate the analysis of the four chords in the blanks provided.

Chords in numbers 1–15 are in root position only:

$B^{\flat}$ Major: I^7 ii^7 iii^7 IV^7 vi^7

1.–10. (R)

1. _____ _____ _____ _____   9. _____ _____ _____ _____

2. _____ _____ _____ _____   10. _____ _____ _____ _____

3. _____ _____ _____ _____   11. _____ _____ _____ _____

4. _____ _____ _____ _____   12. _____ _____ _____ _____

5. _____ _____ _____ _____   13. _____ _____ _____ _____

6. _____ _____ _____ _____   14. _____ _____ _____ _____

7. _____ _____ _____ _____   15. _____ _____ _____ _____

8. _____ _____ _____ _____

Chords in numbers 16–25 include the following inversions:

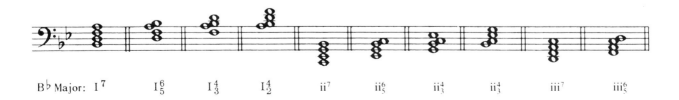

$B^{\flat}$ Major: I^7 I^6_5 I^4_3 I^4_2 ii^7 ii^6_5 ii^4_3 ii^4_3 iii^7 iii^6_5

iii⁴₃   iii⁴₂   IV⁷   IV⁶₅   IV⁴₃   IV⁴₂   vi⁷   vi⁶₅   vi⁴₃   vi⁴₂

16. _____ _____ _____ _____   21. _____ _____ _____ _____

17. _____ _____ _____ _____   22. _____ _____ _____ _____

18. _____ _____ _____ _____   23. _____ _____ _____ _____

19. _____ _____ _____ _____   24. _____ _____ _____ _____

20. _____ _____ _____ _____   25. _____ _____ _____ _____

NAME _____ DATE _____ SECTION _____

11

A. SS Rhythm: The Quartolet in Compound Meter and the Triplet in Simple Meter

I: Procedure

1. Consider each measure as a module to be practiced separately, or as part of a series requested by your instructor.
2. Follow procedures given in Unit 2, Section A, page 23. Work continually for both accuracy and speed—with accuracy taking precedence.

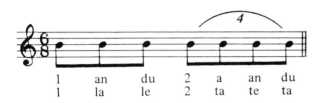

2

3

4

5 Rhythmic Ostinato

6 Upper rhythm repeated twice in lower voice in diminution

B. ET Rhythmic Dictation: The Quartolet

Each exercise consists of a short rhythmic excerpt. Many, but not all of these exercises contain **quartolets,** rhythmic groupings of four which take place in a time span normally given to groupings of three.

Complete the rhythm on a neutral pitch.

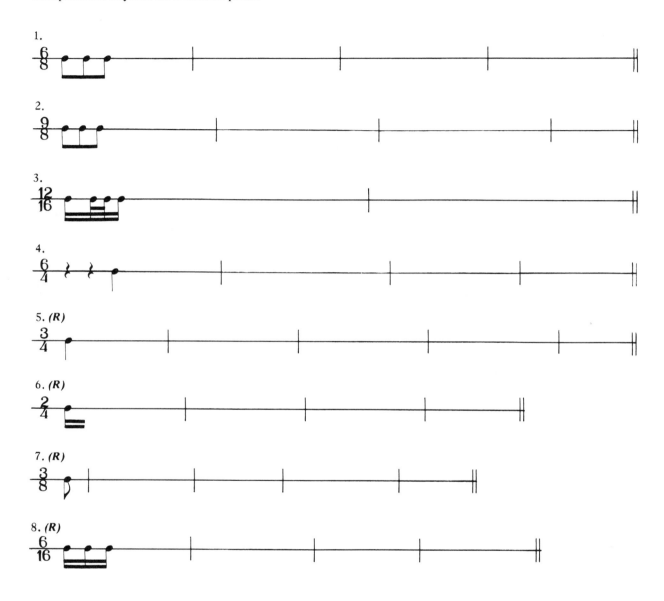

C. SS Diatonic and Chromatic Models for Interval Study
New Intervals: d7, A2
Review: m7, M6, m6, A4

I

Emphasis on intervals of the diminished 7th and augmented 2nd.

The exercises in this section are in g♯ minor and relate to the music of Bach, Haydn, Beethoven, and Wagner. The musical excerpts that correspond with these exercises are quoted in Section D (page 255) of this unit. The models in this chapter relate to fragments in Section D as follows:

Models	Fragments
1	1
2	2
3	3, 4, 5, & 6
4	5
5	7a,b,c,d
6	7a,b,c,d
7	7a,b,c,d
8a	8
8b	8
9	11, 12, 13, 14
10	11, 12, 13, 14, 15

Exercises 1–4

All of the diminished 7ths in these exercises extend from F♯♯ up to E, or E down to F♯♯.

Follow the same procedures as found in previous units. For extra practice, sing exercise 1 in all minor keys, transposing to each new key by P5ths down or P4ths up (see model below). Since the diminished 7th is so neatly framed by the tonic triad, these patterns are excellent for "tossing," as in previous units. Instructors be aware of inappropriately aimed diminished 7ths! Please see the following model:

Exercises 5–7

Exercises 5–7 outline the basic motives of the opening notes of Beethoven's Quartet, op. 133 (The Grand Fugue). Melodic fragments 7a, b, c, and d are from the same quartet. Memorize exercise 7 so you can hear these fragments with your eyes when you reach Section D of this unit.

Exercises 8a and 8b

These exercises focus on the augmented 2nd (F♯♯ down to E, or E up to F♯♯) representing the inversion of the diminished 7th. These augmented 2nds have the same pitches as the diminished 7ths in exercises 1–4. The leading-tone 7th chord in first inversion (vii$_5^{06}$) is indicated in 8b, and emphasizes the symmetry of the diminished 7th chord.

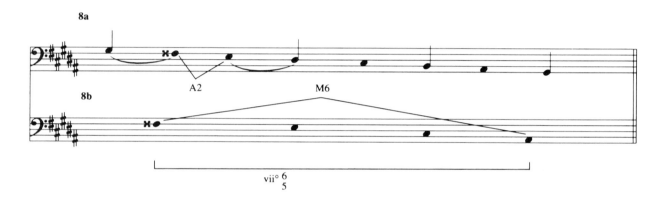

Exercises 9–10

The leading-tone 7th chord, in root position, outlines the diminished 7th chord, and emphasizes the resulting symmetry (minor 3rds or their enharmonic equivalent).

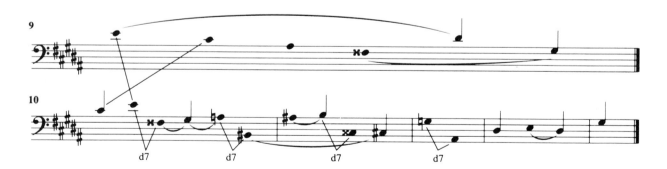

II: Alto and Tenor clefs

a. Alto clef*

Return to the familiar diatonic models of Unit 7, Section C for practice in reading the alto clef. In numbers 1–24, substitute the alto clef for the treble clef and change the key signature (see illustration).

b. Tenor clef*

Return to the models found in Unit 3, Section C for practice in reading the tenor clef. In numbers 1–35, substitute the tenor clef for the given clef and change the key signature (see model).

D. SS Melodic Fragments for Interval Singing
New Intervals: d7, A2

(Note to the instructor: Relate these fragments to drills in Section C, page 253.)

Sing the melodies as written. Most of the diminished 7ths are labeled.

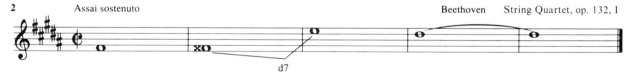

5   Andante   Bach   Three-Part Invention no. 2 (transposed)

d7   d7

6   Moderato   Bach   Two-Part Invention no. 2 (transposed)

d7

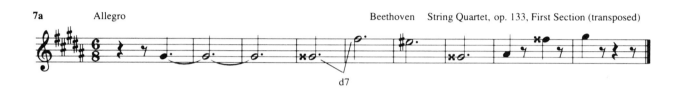

7a   Allegro   Beethoven   String Quartet, op. 133, First Section (transposed)

d7

7b   Allegro   Beethoven   String Quartet, op. 133, First Section (transposed)

d7

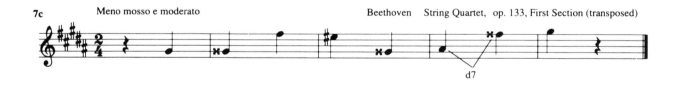

7c   Meno mosso e moderato   Beethoven   String Quartet, op. 133, First Section (transposed)

d7

7d   Allegro   Beethoven   String Quartet, op. 133, First Section (transposed)

8 Andante   Haydn   Piano Sonata XVI: 16 (transposed)

9 Andante   Haydn   Piano Sonata XVI: 12 II (transposed)

10 Lento   Haydn   Song *Dir nah ich mich, nah mich dem Throne* (transposed)

11 Gemächlich bewegt   Wagner   The Twilight of the Gods, Act III, Scene II (transposed)

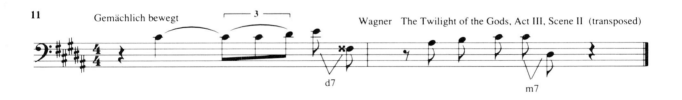

12 Lebhaft   Wagner   The Twilight of the Gods, Act III, Scene I   (transposed)

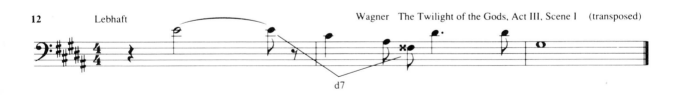

13 Lebhaft   Wagner   The Twilight of the Gods, Act III, Scene I (transposed)

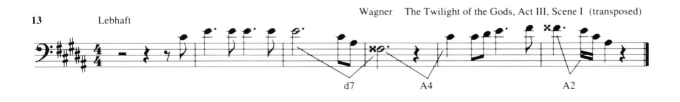

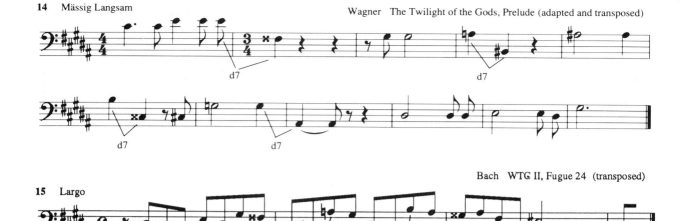

14 Mässig Langsam

Wagner The Twilight of the Gods, Prelude (adapted and transposed)

d7   d7

d7   d7

Bach WTC II, Fugue 24 (transposed)

15 Largo

A4   d7   d7

E. ET Models and Embellishments: 7th-Chord Patterns in Three Voices

1. The model in this section is made up of three voices performing a circle progression or series of ascending fourth root progressions. Sing all parts of this structure before class.
2. Your instructor will play the structure followed by embellishments of that structure.
3. Write the model's embellishments on the numbered staves provided.

Model:

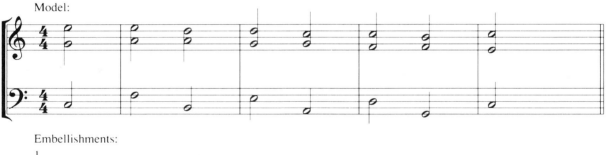

Embellishments:

1

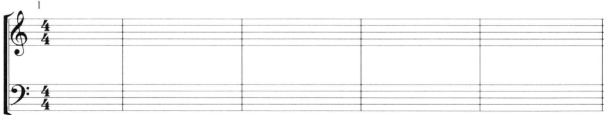

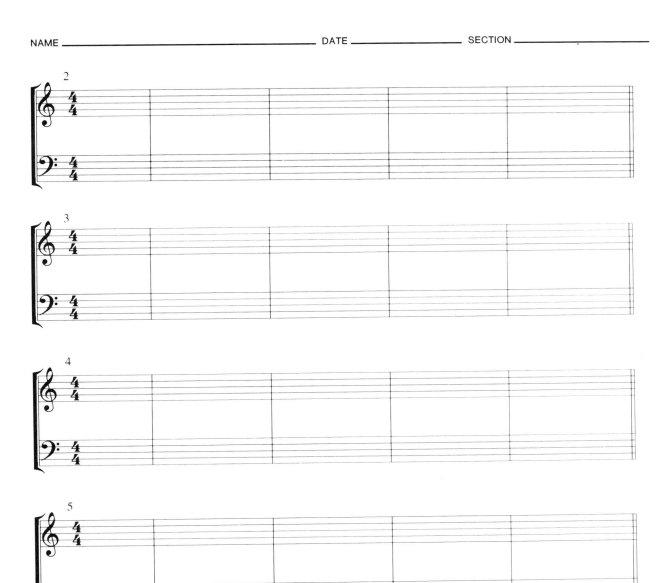

F. SS Melodies (Pentatonic) to Be Sung at Performance Tempo

Procedure for Completing Each Melody

1. All melodies are pentatonic folk songs.
2. The goal of this section is to sing each melody with accuracy at performance tempo on the *first* attempt.
3. Before singing, scan each melody, silently, trying to imagine the sound of each note.
4. When satisfied that the melody is well in mind, you are ready to sing.

1   Allegretto   "The Precious Treasure" from *Songs of the Irish*

From *Songs of the Irish* by Donal O'Sullivan, published by the Mercier Press, 4 Bridge Street, Cork, Ireland. Reprinted by permission.

Folk Song United States

Folk Song United States

Folk Song United States

"Derreen Day" from Songs of the Irish

From *Songs of the Irish* by Donal O'Sullivan, published by the Mercier Press, 4 Bridge Street, Cork, Ireland. Reprinted by permission.

10   Poco pesante

From *Songs of the Irish* by Donal O'Sullivan, published by the Mercier Press, 4, Bridge Street, Cork, Ireland.

G. ET Melodic Dictation: Modulation
to Closely Related Keys

Each exercise consists of a melodic excerpt that modulates to a closely related key.

Complete the melody on the staff in notation.

6. *(R)**

7. *(R)*

8. *(R)*

9. *(R)*

10. *(R)*

**(R)* means recorded.

H. SS Melodies for Careful Study and Review:
Chromatic Alterations, Modulating, and Nonmodulating

I

1.   All of these melodies are sacred and include works by Ellington, Berlioz, and Bach, as well as a Negro Spiritual (Deep River) and two examples of Gregorian Chant (Hymn to St. Thomas Aquinas, *In Paradisum* from the Requiem Mass). The last four examples are from the *Complete Collection of Irish Music* by George Petrie (1789–1866), edited by Charles Villiers Stanford (1902): The Hymn of St. Bernard, The Funeral Cry (Galway, 1840), a Christmas Hymn (Galway), and an Irish Hymn (Londonderry).

2.   For interval practice, select a melody and read it through (without singing), naming the intervals as you read. Try to increase the speed of interval identification as much as you can without sacrificing accuracy.

3.   Then, return to the beginning of the melody and sing it with the solfeggio or number system preferred by your instructor.

DAVID DANCED
Duke Ellington
Copyright © 1963 Famous Music Corporation. Tempo Music for world rights outside of U.S.

1   Brightly

Duke Ellington. Copyright © Music Sales Corporation.

2 Slowly

Duke Ellington. Copyright © Music Sales Corporation.

3 Adagio   Negro Spiritual   "Deep River"

4 Moderato quasi Andantino   Berlioz   Dignare Domine (Prayer), Te Deum

5   Gregorian Chant Hymn to St. Thomas Aquinas

From Mrs. Close   Christmas Carol or Hymn (as sung in the county of Galway)

11 Lento (♩=69)

12 Andante

Irish Hymn Sung on the Dedication of a Chapel Co. of Londonderry

II

1. Among these melodies are keyboard works by Baroque composers and two solo excerpts sung by Emilie in Rameau's opera-ballet *Les Indes galants,* first performed on August 23, 1735.
2. Detailed suggestions for preparing modulating melodies are found in Unit 8, Section H, page 176.

1   Andante

Couperin

2   Andante

Chambonnières

3   Andante

Chambonnières

4   Adagio

Lully

5 Moderato

Byrde

6 Molto vivace

Loeillet

7 Tempête

Rameau (Émilie)   Les Indes galantes

Reproduced by arrangement with the publisher.

8 Tempête

Rameau (Émilie)   Les Indes galantes

Reproduced by arrangement with the publisher.

9   Adagio   Handel   Suite in D Minor, *Sarabande*

10   Andante   Bach   English Suite no. 5, *Sarabande*

11   Allegro piacevole   Bach   English Suite no. 4, *Menuet*

12 Allegro

Bach   Suite No. 1, *Bourrée II*

III

All of the following melodies are excerpts from songs by Brahms.

1 Sehr Lebhaft

Brahms   The Little Drummer's Song, op. 69, no.5

2 Etwas Bewegt

Brahms   Therese, op. 86, I

3 Bewegt und Heimlich

Brahms   Tension, op. 84, no. 5

4 Andante moderato

Brahms   Reminiscences, op. 7, no. 3

5 Allegro

Brahms   Romances from Magelone (No Title), op. 33, no. 5

I. ET Harmonic Intervals

1. Immediately after hearing the interval, sing both pitches: lower to upper for numbers 1–30, and upper to lower for numbers 31–60.
2. Harmonic intervals (both pitches sound together) are considered more difficult than melodic (one note, then the other) because the two tend to fuse into a single, homogenized effect.
3. Separating the two into distinct pitches helps considerably in recognizing and identifying the interval, but remember that this procedure is temporary.
4. Gradually you must learn to identify intervals directly—without going through the intermediary step. Use the crutch for a while, and at the same time keep trying to graduate to the next level.
5. Write the remaining note of the interval on the staff.
6. Write the name of the interval in the blank provided.

The given note is the lower of the two:

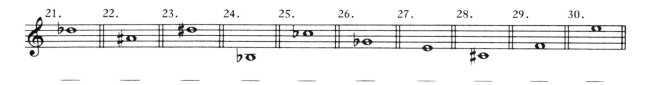

The given note is the higher of the two:

R = 31 – 60

J. SS Ensemble Excerpts: Two, Three, and Four Voices

Procedure

Follow procedures outlined in Unit 4, Section J, page 82.

1   Bach

Moderato Misteriose

Bruckner Christus Factus Est

This excerpt from the eighth verse is from the same motet excerpted in number 1 of this section.

Although the chorale melody is quoted in the alto voice in number 1, it is not found in this section.

3

Bach

4 Lento

Bach   from Var. X (Sei gegrüsset, Jesu gütig)

outer voices

* original is an octave lower

5 Allegretto

Schubert   Fantasy for Piano and Violin, op. 159

The Bb Clarinet sounds a major 2nd lower than written. Use the tenor clef to indicate c'' in singing the transposition. Check your accuracy in the reading of the clarinet part with the harp part. Both lines sound in unison.

K. ET Harmonic Dictation: Dominant 7th Chord in Four-Part Chorale Phrases

Each exercise consists of a chorale phrase.

Numbers	No. of Chords	Position
1–6	4	All in root position
7–12	7	Root position and inversions

1. Indicate the roman-numeral analysis of each triad in the blanks provided.
2. List any nonharmonic tones beneath the harmonic analysis.
3. If the instructor requests it, give the melodic line of both the soprano and bass voices.
4. If the instructor requests it, give the melodic line of both the alto and tenor voices.

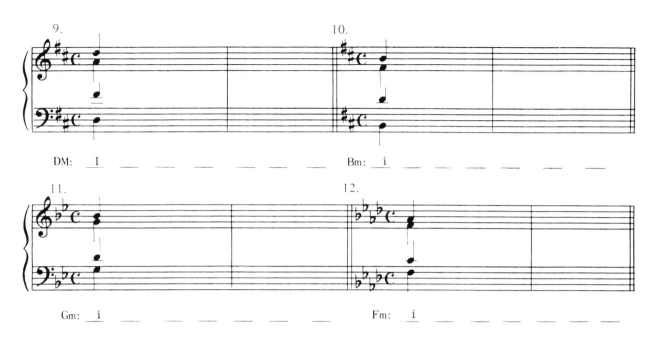

DM: I _____ _____ _____

Bm: i _____ _____ _____

Gm: i _____ _____ _____

Fm: i _____ _____ _____

L. ET Harmonic Function: Secondary Dominants of V and ii

Each exercise consists of a series of four chords in block harmony.

Analyze each of the four chords in the blanks provided.

New chords:

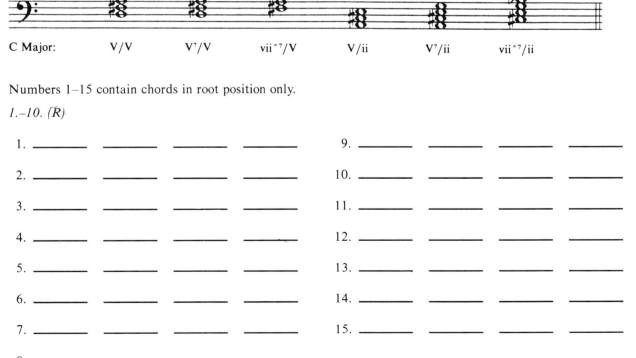

C Major: V/V   V⁷/V   vii°⁷/V   V/ii   V⁷/ii   vii°⁷/ii

Numbers 1–15 contain chords in root position only.

1.–10. (R)

1. _____ _____ _____ _____   9. _____ _____ _____ _____

2. _____ _____ _____ _____   10. _____ _____ _____ _____

3. _____ _____ _____ _____   11. _____ _____ _____ _____

4. _____ _____ _____ _____   12. _____ _____ _____ _____

5. _____ _____ _____ _____   13. _____ _____ _____ _____

6. _____ _____ _____ _____   14. _____ _____ _____ _____

7. _____ _____ _____ _____   15. _____ _____ _____ _____

8. _____ _____ _____ _____

Numbers 16–25 contain inversions.

16. _____ _____ _____ _____   21. _____ _____ _____ _____

17. _____ _____ _____ _____   22. _____ _____ _____ _____

18. _____ _____ _____ _____   23. _____ _____ _____ _____

19. _____ _____ _____ _____   24. _____ _____ _____ _____

20. _____ _____ _____ _____   25. _____ _____ _____ _____

Appendix A: Terms

Term	Translation
A	At, at the
Adagietto	Slower than andante but faster than largo
Adagio	Tempo slower than andante but faster than largo
Agitato	Excited (agitated)
Allegretto	Between allegro and andante
Allegro	Quick tempo
An	In
Andante	Moderate tempo
Andantino	Slightly slower than andante
Animato	In a spirited lively fashion (animated)
Ausdruck	Expression, feeling
Bewegt	Active, with motion, movingly, touchingly
Bewegung	Moving, with movement
Bisschen	Bit
Calmato	Calm
Commodo	At an easy pace
Con	With
Contento	Contented
Di	Of, of a
Die	The
Doch	But
Dolente	Doleful, lamenting
Durch	Through
Ein	A
Einfach	Simple, plain
Energico	With energy
Erzählend	Narrative style
Espress	Expressive
Espressione	Expression
Espressivo	With expression
Etwas	A little, somewhat
Frei	Free
Gavotta	Gavotte (a dance in 4/4 meter, strongly accented)
Gehend	Going, moving
Geschwind	Fast, quick, swift
Giocoso	Humorously, sportively
Gracieux	Gracefully
Heimlich	Secretive
Im	In the
Indolente	Lazy
Innig	Intimate, close
Kokett	Flirtingly (coquet)
Kräftig	Strong, powerful
Langsam	Slow
Larghetto	Slightly faster than largo
Largo	Very slow, broad in character

Term	Translation
Lebhaft	Lively, vivid
Leidenschaftlich	Passion, passionate
Leist	Soft
Lent	Slow
Lento	Slower than andante but faster than larghetto
Ma	But
Maestoso	Majestic, dignified
Mässig	Moderate
Mit	With
Moderato	Moderate pace between andante and allegro
Moto	Motion
Munter	Lively, merry
Mutig	Courageous, undaunted
Nach und nach	Little by little, gradually
Nase	Nose
Nicht	Not
Non	Not
Pesante	Heavy
Piu	More
Poco	Little
Presto	Very fast—faster than allegro
Quasi	Almost
Rasch	Fast (rush)
Rauschend	Exuberant
Rubato	Unsteady tempo—accelerandos and ritardandos
Ruhig	Quiet
Scherzando	Playful
Schnell	Fast, swift, rapid
Sehr	Very
Spirito	Spirit
Stark	Strong
Ton	Tone, sound
Tranquillo	Quietly, tranquil
Tres	Very
Troppo	Too, too much
Un	A
Unruhig	Restless
Vivace	Lively, fast
Volante	Swift
Ziemlich	Rather, fairly, pretty
Zu	To, up to, too

Appendix B: Computer Programs to Accompany This Text

Almost all of the ear training programs in *Introduction to Sightsinging and Ear Training* are found in *Computer Programs to Accompany Ear Training, A Technique for Listening.* This set may be purchased through William C. Brown Co., Publishers. The following chart indicates where each individual assignment may be found. Blanks in the "Disk No." and "Code" columns signify no computer program for that assignment.

Strategies and Applications				Computer Programs	
Unit	*Section*	*Page*	*Title*	*Disk No.*	*Code*
1	B	5	Rhythmic Dictation: Full-Beat and Half-Beat Values	2	R1A
	E	9	Models and Embellishments: Short Melodic Structures	—	—
	G	14	Melodic Dictation: Scalewise (Conjunct Diatonic) Melodies	1	M1C
	I	18	Intervals: m2, M2, m3, M3	5	M1D
	K	20	Chord Identification: Major and Minor Triads	—	—
	L	21	Harmonic Function: I and V Triads	6	H1A
2	B	27	Rhythmic Dictation: Duple and Triple Subdivisions of the Beat	2	R2A
	E	33	Models and Emnbellishments: Short Melodic Structures	—	—
	G	35	Scales: Major Scale and Three Forms of the Minor Scale	—	—
	I	40	Scale Degrees: Single Notes	—	—
	K	42	Chord Identification: Major, Minor, and Diminished Triads	—	—
	L	43	Harmonic Function: I, IV, and V Triads	6	H2A
3	B	48	Rhythmic Dictation: Full-Beat and Half-Beat Values	2	R3B
	E	53	Models and Embellishments: Short Melodic Structures	—	—
	G	55	Melodic Dictation: Dictation Employing m2, M2, m3, M3	1	M2B
	I	60	New Intervals: P5 and P4	5	M2D
	K	62	Chord Identification: Triad Factors in the Soprano	—	—
	L	63	Harmonic Function: I, ii, and V Triads	6	H3A
4	B	67	Rhythmic Dictation: Half-Beat Values in Syncopation	2	R4B
	E	71	Models and Embellishments: Descending 3rds in Two Voices	—	—
	G	76	Melodic Dictation: Using m2, M2, m3, M3, P4, P5	1	M3B
	I	81	Intervals: Review (m2, M2, m3, M3, P4, P5)	5	M3E
	K	84	Chord Identification: Major and Minor Triad Positions	—	—
	L	85	Harmonic Function: Among the I, ii, IV, and V Triads	6	H4A

Appendix C: Audio Tapes to Accompany Introduction to Sightsinging and Ear Training

Chapter	Section	Tape Side	Announced As
1	B	1	Unit 1, Rhythm, Section A
1	G	1	Unit 1, Melody, Section C
1	I	1	Unit 1, Melody, Section D
1	L	1	Unit 1, Harmony, Section A
2	B	1	Unit 2, Rhythm, Section A
2	G	1	Unit 3, Melody, Section D
2	L	1	Unit 2, Harmony, Section A
3	B	2	Unit 3, Rhythm, Section B
3	G	1	Unit 2, Melody, Section B
3	I	1	Unit 2, Melody, Section D
3	K	1	Unit 1, Harmony, Section C
3	L	2	Unit 3, Harmony, Section A
4	B	2	Unit 4, Rhythm, Section B
4	G	1	Unit 3, Melody, Section B
4	I	2	Unit 3, Melody, Section E
4	K	1	Unit 1, Harmony, Section D
4	L	2	Unit 4, Harmony, Section A
5	B	3	Unit 5, Rhythm, Section A
5	G	2	Unit 4, Melody, Section A
5	L	3	Unit 5, Harmony, Section A
6	B	3	Unit 6, Rhythm, Section A
6	G	3	Unit 5, Melody, Section A
6	I	2	Unit 4, Melody, Section D
6	K	2	Unit 3, Harmony, Section D
6	L	3	Unit 6, Harmony, Section A
7	B	4	Unit 7, Rhythm, Section B
7	G	3	Unit 6, Melody, Section A
7	L	4	Unit 7, Harmony, Section A
8	B	4	Unit 8, Rhythm, Section A
8	G	3	Unit 7, Melody, Section B
8	I	3	Unit 6, Melody, Section D
8	K	2	Unit 3, Harmony, Section B
8	L	4	Unit 8, Harmony, Section A
9	B	5	Unit 9, Rhythm, Section A
9	G	4	Unit 8, Melody, Section A
9	I	3	Unit 5, Melody, Section D
9	K	2	Unit 4, Harmony, Section C
9	L	5	Unit 10, Harmony, Section A

Chapter	Section	Tape Side	Announced As
10	B	5	Unit 10, Rhythm, Section A
10	G	5	Unit 9, Melody, Section A
10	I	6	Unit 11, Melody, Section D
10	K	4	Unit 7, Harmony, Section C
10	L	6	Unit 12, Harmony, Section A
11	B	6	Unit 11, Rhythm, Section B
11	G	5	Unit 11, Melody, Section A
11	I	5	Unit 9, Melody, Section D
11	L	7	Unit 13, Harmony, Section A

Index